DISCOVER PURPOSE

The Anthology

Resources to Guide You
from Pain to Purpose

© Evelyn Whitebear, 2017

Andrea Nicole, Sam Lyndley
&
The Discover Your Purpose Authors

Illustrated by Evelyn Whitebear

Disclaimer
All the contributions contained within this publication are of the nature of personal experience only, and are not in any way directed as individual advice guaranteed to work in the same way it has for the author. The intent is to offer a journey that provides a wider range of choices now and in the future, recognising that we all have widely diverse circumstances and viewpoints.
Should any reader choose to make use of the information herein, this is their decision, and the author and printer do not assume any responsibilities whatsoever under any conditions or circumstances. It is highly recommended that the reader operate an open mind and heart whilst accompanying the authors on their respective journeys.

By
Jo Gomme

Looking through Facebook I found this group,
'Discover Your Purpose'; sounded quite good.

It was for likeminded souls
To uncover their goals,
To share what they know
And teach as they grow.

Discover Your Purpose seemed to be,
The place where I could be, whole-heartedly me.

What wonderful people I found in this group,
And then I heard they were writing a book!

An Anthology no less, a collection of stories,
From each of the members, tales of guts and of glories.

I cannot write, my story is flat,
My time with a pen is just doodles; That's that!

Then something triggered me, and told me to write,
And so I started early, one October night.

Within a few hours I had written it down,
A life story, a poem from then until now.

To this group I owe gratitude for helping me find,
My way back to my path in flow, without grind.

To Sam a huge thank you for sharing your time,
For starting this group and inviting us in.

To Andrea - Wow! A huge thankyou indeed!
For writing was something that I didn't see!

My thanks to all who are part of this group,
And gratitude to everyone who buys this book.

There is no greater cause than helping others.
With our group and this book that is exactly what we do,
Much love,
Jo Gomme
xxx

Here is what our stories cover:
Abuse
Adoption
Angels
Anger
Anxiety
Aromatherapy
Asthma
Bullying
Cognitive Behaviour Therapy
Counselling
Depression
Earth Angels
Grief
Homosexuality
IBS
Infertility
Infidelity
Loss
OCD
Pregnancy
PTSD
Reiki
Surrogacy

DEDICATIONS – from Andrea Nicole

I am deeply indebted to my Mum & Dad, Eileen Marina & William James, who within their own professions were hard workers, passing their strong work ethic onto me. You never saw me fully in my element Dad and I miss you terribly, but I know you are around me all the time, guiding me to be my best me, so that I can leave a legacy we're all proud of. I love you Daddy. Mum, you are the strongest person I know. There's such a wealth of love in your heart for everyone you meet. You are my inspiration and I hope I can become one iota of who you are. Mummy, I love you 2lb of sugar – and more!

For my Brother Darrel, you have experienced so much pain in your life, even sharing some of mine. You'll never know how much I love you, I just hope that someday you find the kind of love that suits you.

Martin, you said you were proud of me for donating my time and building this book; those words mean the world to me. I love you with all my heart and soul, and thank you for patiently supporting me through many hours of editing. Thank you for being you.

I have two Sam's in my life, Sam Lyndley and my cousin Sam Lafferty. You have both been by my side to guide and help me; Yes, I've known you just a short time Sam Lyndley – as my trusted Mentor – and yet, I am indebted to you for helping me find my truth. As for my Cousin Sam Lafferty, you have been my friend and the Sister I never had for all of your life, being nine years younger than me. Thank you for everything you do, and for giving me another Brother and 3 beautiful boy-babes in Paul, Flynn, Beau and Drew. A magical family.

Thank you to Harry Singha, Anita 'may the laugh be with you' Langley, Karen Shaw, Lisa Page and Mo Latin, who each believed in me as a Writer/Editor/Mentor. Thankyou Mike Fisher of BAAM and the Balanced Minds team, for your valuable work. Indeed, there are many more people I would like to thank for being in my life, and you certainly know who you are. Love you all.

Andrea Nicole

DEDICATIONS – from Sam Lyndley

Firstly, I'd like to share my deep appreciation and praise for Andrea Nicole, for coming up with the wonderful idea of compiling an 'Anthology' and asking us all to be involved. You have dedicated so much of your time and energy for this to happen and if it wasn't for you Andrea, this book would never have come about!

I am also forever grateful to my partner in life Jeremy Spirit, for your generous heart, loving support and unwitting belief in me.

For my boys, Tom and Ben, who are my life, my world and my biggest teachers, I love you both.

My Mum and Dad, Yvonne & Fred, for making me the person I am today and being there for me when the chips are down and to my brother Rich, for being the kindest Brother I could have wished for.

I'd also like to mention my Grandmothers Mary and Winifred, who were both a constant source of love throughout my life. My Nanny Ruddick, as I liked to call her (Winifred), had a very difficult life and experienced such loss and pain over the years. I have so much compassion and empathy towards her and I thank both my Grandmothers for laying the path for me, so I can walk as the strong independent woman I am today.

And of course, last but not least, for the lady that took my hand all those years ago and led me back home to me, Kate Maryon. Thank you!

There have been so many beautiful souls who have touched my life in so many ways over the years; you know who you are! The special ones that give your time and your love so freely and with such generosity, my Aunty Maureen is indeed one of those special souls, as are my best friends Gina, Julie, Mandy, Debs, Donna and Belinda; I love you all.

Sam Lyndley

"Do not be afraid of change;
it's a part of life and a way for you to grow
and explore different options."

Cath B

CONTENTS

FOREWORD

On Behalf of
The Mental Health Foundation

The Mental Health Foundation is a wonderful charity which is conducting research into issues faced by many people daily.

This is why we have chosen this particular charity to receive the entire proceeds from the sale of our books on Amazon.

This is what they have to say:

"Our vision is for a world with good mental health for all. Our mission is to help people to thrive through understanding, protecting and sustaining their mental health.

The social challenge of our time is to reverse the growing level of mental ill health.

Good mental health is fundamental to thriving in life. It is the essence of who we are and how we experience the world. Yet, compared to physical health, so little is commonly known about mental ill health and how to prevent it. That must change.

The Mental Health Foundation is the UK's charity for everyone's mental health. With prevention at the heart of what we do, we aim to find and address the sources of mental health problems. We must make the same progress for the health of our minds that we have achieved for the health of our bodies. And when we do, we will look back and think that this was our time's greatest contribution to human flourishing."

"Every year, our work in mental health changes thousands of people's lives. We can do that because of the generosity and kindness of our supporters. There is so much more that can be done. Together we are tackling one of the defining challenges of our time for this generation and the next."

Jenny Edwards CBE
Chief Executive
Mental Health Foundation

The Mental Health Foundation is dedicated to finding and addressing the sources of mental health problems.

We invite you to join them here:
http://www.mentalhealth.org.uk

ACKNOWLEDGMENTS

As Editor of this important book, I am hugely grateful to everyone who has contributed. The Authors here are business people who took time out of their busy days to write about their challenges and what steps they took to overcome them, so that we might help others with their struggles.

Were it not for these contributors, there would not be an Anthology, so thank you to so many wonderful people.

Just as important to this Anthology is Sam Lyndley, who made it possible for us to come together in harmony in her wonderful 'Discover Your Purpose' Facebook group. Without this pivotal step, it's likely that none of us would be here in companionable friendship - and neither would the book!

Many thanks to Evelyn Whitebear who is an amazingly talented artist and who has provided all the imagery, including building the cover.

We all appreciate the Mental Health Foundation in providing such creative resources to help the public with their mental health challenges and therefore the entire proceeds of each book will be donated to this worthy charity, who have endorsed our book by writing a Foreword.

I personally wish to acknowledge the vital work of all life coaches, spiritual healers and anyone caring for the physical and mental health of others through their vocation.

Finally, I wish to thank the families and friends of all our Authors who have supported us throughout our journeys and through the intense production of this book.

My love and thanks to you all.
Andrea Nicole
xxx

"Do not be ashamed of your story.

Write it, share it and tell the world about it.

Your story has made you who you are."

Cath B

FIRST PREFACE
By
Andrea Nicole

Born in 1960, I was raised by Parents with their own individual issues. I've always loved them both dearly, and know that my life growing up was perfect – although with its own challenges; like my Mother, I was shy with little confidence. I inherited this as part of my upbringing and carried it with me for many years.

People often viewed me as stuck-up; I was simply an awkward introvert. I never really grew up, feeling odd because I felt like a child and couldn't identify with many adults, preferring my own company or that of hyperactive children who would see me as a pushover – and do just that! ☺

I can remember going to a family party in my 20's and to avoid the adults drinking and smoking in the kitchen, talking about politics and things that didn't interest me, I ended up brawling on the floor with their young children, having the time of our lives. I often felt socially awkward because I just didn't fit in; too old physically to play with the kids and too young mentally to relate with the adults.

I ruined relationships with my childish or child-like ways; being responsible was not for me, although my quiet side screamed dull and mature. This went on for years - decades in fact - before I really understood that I didn't fit in because I was mixing with people who didn't understand me.

It took the death of my Father in 2004 to take me to the deep depths of depression before I began to wake up and realise that something in me needed to shift, BIG TIME!

Waking up to my inner light and purpose has been a slow process for me and has required a good chunk of financial investment in terms of coaches, seminars and books.

At the age of 44, I'd lost my Dad, my relationship was going nowhere and my work was unfulfilling. Two years later, still stuck but with the addition of anger ruling and intruding on my life, I came across a book called 'Notes from a Friend' by Tony Robbins. I purchased this online from an events company, who called me a couple of weeks later to offer me a seat at Tony Robbins' London event: UPW: Unleash the Power Within. I had some reservations and resistance, but eventually, I managed to find the £300 and attended the 4-day action-packed seminar. It was my first real investment in shaping my mind, through which I found a group of friends I still have today.

I didn't stop there, as I met Anita Langley who was active in the YES Group London, which was founded by Karl Pearsall, both UPW participants. Attending monthly meetings, I kept the momentum going, learning how to find my best me, and how the power of intention could reshape my life. I volunteered to crew for the organisation, the following UPW event and other similar events, where my willingness to interact and grow earned me a wide network of incredibly inspirational people. I felt like I was flying!

Things don't always continue the way you imagine they might and in my naivete I was totally unaware I was heading for another crash. All I had done was gloss over my challenges; I had so much more to learn. In terms my Mum would declare, I'd put a brave face on to manage my life and lifestyle!

The anger that began as a tiny flame of injustice at the cause of my Dad's asbestos-related death, bubbled beneath the surface, fuelled by an opening of my mind to the many atrocities that were happening world-wide. I was engulfed with bitterness, sandwiched between bouts of positivity; I roller-coasted like this for years.

In late 2009 I met a man who was to change my world as I knew it, with a New Year's Eve kiss at midnight sealing my fate. Through this passionate relationship I became a live-in Auntie to his 10-year old Nephew who had sadly lost his Mum to Cancer, aged just 42.

Was I aware that as a stand-in maternal figure, just one year into a new relationship, that I was going to lose my identity, my mind and fall deeper and deeper into nothingness? Of course not! But I did anyway!

Such a lot of issues reared up for me; a lack of self-confidence and self-esteem, anger and anxiety because I didn't feel I fitted in to this completely new tribe, causing a green-eyed monster to dominate my existence. My sensitive heart was in pain, my loved ones and extended family members felt it too.

At the ripe age of 51, never able to bear children of my own to full term, I realised that parenting required a lot more than just being a friend. I was no expert; all I had to give was love, but I could find none for me as I felt a failure, so the love going out was minimal! (You'll understand this if you've ever heard that you can't love another until you love yourself – which is true by the way!)

To those I have inadvertently hurt, I apologise. It has never been my intention to hurt anyone. Yet in the process, it was me I hurt the most!

My inner child has always yearned to be heard and in denying her what I feel is everyone's birth-right, my irresponsible actions have almost cost me what I crave most; love!

Having worked for 4 years with the beautiful Lisa Page from Soul Satisfaction for Women, I discovered a Facebook Group called Discover Your Purpose, facilitated by the empathic intuitive Sam Lyndley.

Joining was mandatory rather than a conscious decision and soon I was diving deeper than ever into my psyche. It is here and bang up to date that I can share with you the massive leap I have taken to truly discovering my purpose, through Sam's honest and fearless coaching.

Mentoring me through some very hesitant steps to realising my true skills and engaging with my own intuition, Sam guided me with a light brighter than my own, to open a portal I always had access to but wasn't ready for. She opened my eyes to my own light!

My evolving business as a commercial and creative writer, editor and writing mentor, has since provided a source and sense of fulfilment I have long been searching for; it was there all the time and it feels wonder-full...!!!

How inspiring and satisfying to realise that my purpose has always been to help others. It's always been within me, I just didn't know it.

The enlightened members of our purposeful group have all been part of my growth in confidence and self-esteem, each one an incredible source of wisdom derived from their own challenging experiences. Putting this Anthology together is my gift to them, along with the wider recipients of this collection of works.

By purchasing this book, you are helping to fund the vital activities of The Mental Health Foundation which offers help and a safe space to those in need of stability and guidance; a charity I have utilised and learned from throughout my own years in turmoil.

Please join the members of the 'Discover Your Purpose' Facebook Group in offering much-needed support to the charity's vital resources, whilst also opening your own mind to what's possible for you and yours. Perhaps you'd even like to pay this intention forward.

There's never been a better time to support the mental health of our nation; I thank you wholeheartedly for your valuable contribution.

With love,
Andrea Nicole
xxx

http://www.andreanicole.co.uk

SECOND PREFACE
By
Sam Lyndley

'In memory of Nicky, who lost his way through poor
mental health'

Don't judge my path
if you haven't walked
my journey
                                        Buddhist quote

The story of 'Discover Your Purpose – The Anthology'

When Andrea asked me to write a preface for this book, I knew I
needed to tell the story of how this group of sensitive, intuitive,
gifted souls came about.

I had been on my own healing journey for many years and only more
recently in July 2016, shifted my focus into offering my services as an
intuitive healer and mentor in a professional manner. I absolutely
loved what I was doing and the only thing that felt missing in my life
was my tribe. I needed to feel connection with other likeminded
souls where I could freely express myself.

I soon realised my tribe wasn't too far away and it was during
December 2016 that my Facebook group 'Discover your Purpose' was
born, she needed to be brought to life and I couldn't do this on my
own, so luckily the word spread and others were called to join me.
We began to open up and talk about our healing journeys, the pain
we'd experienced and it felt good to share our stories in a safe space
away from judgement and the fear of persecution.

From here, miracles started to happen; I noticed many of the group, through sharing their own difficult experiences, started to deeply heal and move forward in their life. I was truly inspired with a huge sense of fulfilment.

During this past year, the miracles have continued with members stepping out of their comfort zone and into the life they'd been dreaming of for so long.

Some of the group members have even gone on to have their first book published; others have created spiritual businesses and practices, held retreats and online workshops. Being brave and facing their fears has become part of their daily life and it's changing lives, not only their own but it has a knock-on effect; as we heal, we heal others. It has been a great time of transformation and growth. This clearly shows me the power of community, which I believe so many of us have lost over time, and is evidently crucial in our wellbeing and ability to heal.

Andrea, who I have co-authored this book with, has been a big player within our group right from the beginning, she has always led from the heart, freely sharing her experience and advice, helping one of our members to write a book and become published whilst working with more of us to do the same. Andrea is a true inspiration; many of us have benefited from her wisdom, vision and infectious playful energy.

Indeed, this wondrous book came about because of Andrea and her quest to encourage more and more of us to share our poignant stories so that others can heal, through recognising they aren't alone in their struggles. This is a powerfully healing message in itself and will no doubt facilitate healing for so many of you who have the pleasure of reading this anthology; this treasure trove of curveballs that life has thrown at us.

With my deepest love and compassion dear reader, enjoy, digest and please always know that you are never alone on your healing journey.

With love, Sam x

http://www.facebook.com/discoveryourpurpose
http://www.samlyndley.com

"You will notice when your heart and your soul are one.

You feel balanced and focused.
You do not make hasty decisions.
You make choices for you and not someone else.
Your decisions are clear and
never based on fear."

Cath B

"Use your life experiences to help and inspire others. What you have been through matters; you now have a tremendous skill and gift to support those in need."

Cath B

"YOU ARE A HEALER!"
By
Sam Lyndley

As a little girl I always sensed I was different, as in, life felt harsh to me. I felt lost and disconnected for many years and no doubt for many of our readers, you will have a similar story to tell...the story of 'the sensitive'!

As a young girl I didn't understand why I often felt the need to retreat and be alone and I'm sure many of my family and friends thought I was very strange. This only reinforced my feeling of not fitting in which I have carried forward into my adult life and is the reason I mainly spend my time with other 'sensitive' souls who I find easy to be around.

Being a sensitive person can mean that we become overwhelmed very quickly and need to withdraw. Explaining this need to be alone to someone who isn't sensitive, in my experience, can be painful as they often see this as a weakness rather than the gift it is. But this is what makes us who we are; the trusted 'go to' person for those in need and we are the best healers, counsellors, coaches, mentors and therapists because we listen deeply, we sense other people's pain without even speaking it, we are the empaths of life!

I grew up as a shy girl, a little bit on the chubby side with very unruly hair, I'd often be called "straw head", which gave me a complex and for years. I didn't even wash my own hair, instead I'd take myself off to the hairdressers each week so they could make it look super sleek for me. What I now know though, is that I have Leo rising in my astrological chart which gives me my lion's hair, so these days I choose to embrace my beautiful wild hair rather than trying to tame it!

I had no real aspirations whilst growing up apart from trying to fathom out where the hell I was, I felt I'd landed on an alien planet which I didn't really didn't care for or particularly understand and I remember hoping and praying that someone familiar would come and save me and take me back home. They never did of course, but I saved myself much later in life as I matured and began to understand my own needs by caring for the sensitive soul that I am, giving myself the gentleness and love that nurtures me well.

My school years were quite painful, I didn't really enjoy school, as I always seemed to attract friends who were bullies and again they seemed to see my kindness as a weakness and would walk all over me, I found this behaviour hard to manage, as I didn't enjoy confrontation, so I'd just shrink back rather than stand up for myself and again I found myself feeling lonely and out on a limb.

I loved animals though and spending time with the many different ones that I had over the years was a great therapy for a sensitive child, I had a cat, rabbit, guinea pigs, dog and pony. Looking back, I was very good at manifesting these animals into my life; I still have the ability to manifest and when I put my mind to it, it happens really quickly. Sometimes I just need to remind myself of this.

I believe we all have this ability but most of us buy into 'lack' rather than 'abundance'. It's easy to see how the law of attraction works just by looking around; the rich find it easy to get richer and the poor find it easy to become poorer. The difficulty is in breaking out of the old patterns and way of thinking. It can be done though, and I have seen it happen regularly. By shifting our mindset and backing this up with action, miracles manifest.

All was quiet on the spirit front until I was aged 18; unknown to me, spirit were just about to enter my life and all was about to change. I was living with my boyfriend at the time and things weren't going particularly well between us.

We were living in an old house and although I wasn't aware of spirit at this point in my life, I just 'knew' something felt somewhat eerie and spooky, so when my partner would go off to work early in the morning I'd lock my bedroom door and go back to sleep.

On one particular morning, I'd locked the door as usual and drifted back off to sleep. When I awoke, I was hit by terror, my bedroom door was wide open and the wardrobe drawers were pulled out.

I screamed out of my bedroom window at a lady who was walking by, to come round to the back of my house to where my front door was. I was petrified that 'someone' was in my house...I left that day, my relationship coming to an end...*just as spirit had wanted!*

This was just the beginning of many strange goings on, wherever I chose to live, spirit would follow. I didn't sleep for years after this event because I was too scared to go to sleep as I'd always wake to a figure in my room, especially in the doorway for some reason.

I didn't speak to anyone about this part of my life as I wouldn't have even known who to turn to and I was worried people would think I was going mad. It was only when my eldest son Tom was seeing Kate, a homoeopath, who asked if I was ok, that I brought it up. I must have looked tired; I said I hadn't slept for years and she invited me to come and see her on my own. I booked an appointment and found myself opening up for the first time, about what I was seeing at night. Bless her, she gently explained that I was seeing 'spirit'. This was a pinnacle moment in my life; everything started to make sense and I remember feeling such relief. Relief that I wasn't actually losing my mind.

Fast forward a few years and I found myself attending an evening of mediumship with a friend whose brother had passed over to spirit and she was hoping to connect with him. During the demonstration, the medium walked over to me and said, "You are a Healer". Four words that changed my life forever.

This message was a powerful one and I started questioning my life; why am I here? I'd always felt there must be a reason for my existence, but I had no idea what it was. I was intrigued by the medium's message and went on to become a Reiki Healer, which led me on a journey of self-discovery and an unwitting desire to seek the truth in everything and everyone, which as you can imagine wasn't always as well received as I'd have liked.

As time went on I started to notice that I'm very intuitive and I would just know what people were thinking or feeling before they would even speak. This is a gift of course, but it also brings its own challenges, as being a sensitive person, it can overwhelm me at times, especially when I can pick up other people's negativity towards me. I've had to learn how to hone this energy and I now use it in a positive way to help the people I work with.

Around this time, I found myself in a book shop having a browse around and I was drawn to a book called 'Be Your Own Psychic' written by the author Sherron Mayes. When I got home I picked up the book and my hands literally started pulsating and getting really hot. Once I started reading, I couldn't put the book down; I knew this stuff, it was as if the wisdom within me was being awakened. Everything the author wrote about made total sense to me. From this place another world opened up and my intuition and psychic abilities started to quickly develop and spirit would come in close whenever they needed to.

I'll always remember the time I had a lady from the village where I lived, come to my house for healing with her teenage daughter who had been suffering with eating disorders. The daughter was beautiful, but she couldn't see it herself, she was caked in makeup and had very low self-esteem. As I began healing, I could sense the energy in the room change, the music stopped, the candles went out and as I went to put my hands on this young lady's head, I felt a force push me away. I quickly picked up that there was an energy attached to this girl. I shared what I was picking up and the mother explained that her daughter had been one half of twins conceived by her, and she had lost the other baby early on in her pregnancy.

As soon as the mother had recognised the spirit as the child she'd lost, the energy shifted and I was able to continue healing. The spirit moved on that day and the next time I saw the teenage girl walk past my house I didn't see a trace of makeup and when I spoke to her

Mum, she explained that her daughter was doing really well and felt like a different person.

Spirit will always try and guide us to the person that can help, they have done this for me on many occasions, like the time with the Homeopath and Medium I spoke about earlier.

When someone is ready to heal, spirit will do everything to assist; we just need to recognise the signs.

One of these times was when a lady called Mandy had recently moved close by to where I lived, I was told that she was severely depressed and in a bad way, so I asked a friend to drop a note through this lady's door inviting her to come and see me for some healing. Little did I know this was to be one of those meetings that would stay with me forever. Mandy went on to tell me about her Father's recent sudden death; how the shock had brought on cancer in her kidney and she was suffering with terrible post-natal depression and was coping by taking high doses of anti-depressants.

I took Mandy upstairs into my little healing room and as she lay on the couch, the whole room lit up in the brightest colour yellow I'd ever seen, I couldn't believe my eyes; it was the most beautiful Angel, she enveloped Mandy in her wings as I laid my hands on her and sent healing, and just as I did so, I felt spirit for the first time ever step into my body, somehow it felt safe and I trusted all was as it should be. This spirit was Mandy's father who had come to give his daughter healing.

 As we went to say our goodbyes, she explained that she had always been interested in the spiritual world and she had a collection of crystals from long ago but they were packed away in the loft somewhere; she said she felt guided to hunt them out.

This was the beginning of Mandy's healing journey and her way back to 'feeling' again, allowing life back in after what had been a very scary time for her. She healed very quickly and we became good friends. Together we ran a little healing clinic on a Wednesday evening; she would use her crystals and I'd use my intuition and link with spirit and together we were a great twosome. Through our love of working together we collaborated in bringing many spiritual fayres and events to our local community, this was a fun time and we met lots of lovely people.

It never ceases to amaze me, the ability mankind has, to heal from such terrible circumstances, be it through loss, ill health or emotional breakdowns. We seem to have this innate force within us that drives us to recover and at times thrive in spite of the pain we have experienced and when this doesn't happen, we can always reach out to someone else who can be the light for us until we are ready to be it for ourselves.

It was during December 2015 that I finally decided it was time to wholeheartedly step into the shoes of the Healer and Mentor. I'd been dreaming this vision in for so many years with no idea how it would happen. I'd frequently ask myself, "How do people financially support themselves whilst being a healer?" Everywhere I looked all I could see were healers doing what they love, but most of them were financially broke. I wanted to create a new story, one where we can do what we love but also be paid well. This was my mission and still is to a degree.

I left my job as a Lettings New Business Manager which I'd foolishly taken on in a moment of madness after being peeved at spirit for letting me down, or at least I thought they had. Three years prior to this, I'd sold my busy, very stressful but successful Letting Agency to be of service and I thought spirit would guide me to my purpose, but oh no, it wasn't meant to be at this time; little did I know I still had much more to learn!

First of all, my Brother was taken very ill with double pneumonia and was in intensive care for weeks. I was heartbroken as we were told he probably wouldn't make it through the first night. Thank God he did and I'm eternally grateful for all the support and healing from dear friends and healers at this time.

Only a couple of months later I found out I had pre-cancerous cells in my cervix which took weeks and weeks for results to come back and then I had to wait to receive treatment and then more results. This took 6 months in total and at the end of it, on top of the worry about my Brother I was left feeling frazzled and mentally and emotionally burnt out from years of anxiety and overwhelm that had pushed my nervous system to its limit.

This was a huge wake up call for me and forced me to take some time out to recover. In all honesty it probably took me about three years to start feeling well again. This was indeed another lesson that taught me well; we can't take our mental and physical health for granted. It's also helped me to recognise burn out in others and I always try and steer people away from making the same mistakes that I did, but as a healer I understand we are all here on our own path and we have our own experiences that we need to work through, so we can give guidance. It is none of our business however, if they choose not to take it.

It came to my awareness that my womb had been struggling for years. I'd suffered with large fibroids, bladder and pelvic infections and excruciating periods. These were so bad that I'd been numbing down the pain with painkillers and the contraceptive pill, but this was just a case of putting a plaster over a huge wound; I was only dealing with the symptoms but not the root cause.

The truth was, I'd abused this area of my life for years, allowing the same kind of guy in who had no business being there; guys who didn't respect me, but who due to my insecurities about who I was coupled with a deep fear of abandonment, I kept attracting into my life. Little did I know this had been causing huge problems in my womb.

It's only now, one year on from having the all clear after my treatment that I fully understand how much my body was struggling. I now feel such compassion towards the younger me, the Sam who didn't know any better or have much awareness. The younger me who thought that to feel safe, it meant having a guy by her side, even if it was the wrong guy. This makes me sad to think of all the years I wasted, but the truth is, we wake up when we wake up!

At the beginning of 2017, I was called to move from my home town of Wiltshire to be close to the sea in Cornwall. I wasn't sure why I was called to move but the message was crystal clear, so I rented out my home and moved to Falmouth with my partner Jer. This was a huge feat for me, as I have two adult sons back home that I love dearly, and who I knew I'd miss terribly. But I trusted my intuition and settled into my new life in Cornwall.

The first few months were difficult at times as I felt homesick but deep down I just knew I was here for a reason and it didn't take long to realise what that was. It came to me in a dream; I was fast asleep, but something strange happened, I was witnessing my dream. I was in a hospital talking to a little girl; I didn't know who she was, nor her Father and she kept holding her belly and seemed in pain. I walked off and asked a doctor what was wrong with her; he said she has cervical cancer. I was distraught in my dream, so upset for this little girl. I then asked spirit why I was being shown this dream and they said, "Because the cancer will come back".

I immediately woke feeling pretty shaken. The first thing I did the next day was book an appointment to have another smear test and travelled all the way to Wiltshire for the procedure. But when I arrived they wouldn't do it, it had been too soon since my previous one. Surprisingly I was ok with this, as whilst I'd been sat waiting, a message had come; it was time for **me** to heal my womb, or else yes, maybe the cancer would come back.

So, this is where I am right now, sat at my desk, writing my contribution to the Anthology, living by the sea, enjoying the peace and quiet and taking each day as it comes, never quite knowing where this healing journey is taking me but trusting I'm exactly where I need to be.

This is the reason I was called to Cornwall, I wouldn't have heard this message if I hadn't moved here; I was always so busy, but here I am, with the time and energy this journey requires of me. I didn't see this coming, but I'm so pleased it did. My feeling is, the dream I had that night may well have saved my life.

I've recently stopped taking my contraceptive pill, after years of purposely stopping myself from having a period. This is something I never thought I'd be able to achieve because of the pain and flooding I'd previously experienced, but I've been able to do this through lots of healing and energy work and giving my womb the attention she needs and as I gently walk this new path, I'm sharing my journey with other women so that they can also release past trauma and pain and begin their own womb healing journey.

I'm hoping that sometime in the near future I will write the whole story of my life. I'm experiencing some resistance, but I'm not sure why. Maybe because I'm not proud of all of it, and I'm sure this is true for many of us, but the desire to help others who are also ready to heal is powerful and I feel I'm being prepared to share my story.

I look forward to this next chapter of my life; I've always felt that writing would call me and it seems it has. No doubt Andrea who I've co-authored this book with, has come into my life for a reason. As I always say there are no 'coincidences' in life, in fact the co-incidence of us all coming together is proof of fate itself.

My journey so far has been an extraordinary one in so many ways; I've witnessed so much pain and so much joy, total polarity at times within my own life and my clients, friends and family. I question how much difference one person can make in a world where there seems to be so much suffering, but then I only have to look around to see all the other healers that are awakening and also hearing the call, "*You are a healer*".

With love,
Sam x

http://facebook.com/discoveryourpurpose
http://www.samlyndley.com

"When you tap into the wisdom of your soul; you will find your path to enlightenment."

Cath B

GRIEF, DEPRESSION & ANGER;
HOW I WORKED THROUGH MY PAIN
By
Andrea Nicole

It's very painful to admit and even share this in the written word, however I'm certain I'm not alone in feeling as if I was 'Born Angry'.

Growing up, I have some frustrating memories:

❖ *When I was 2 or 3, I used to hold the soft skin in the hollow of my Mum and Gran's throats and 'twiddle it' hard between my small fingers, whilst gritting my teeth.*

❖ *Mum used to sing to me whilst I stood on her lap holding her hands and rocking back and forth; I would pull on her saying, "Faster, faster". Such were the frustrating memories I have growing up.*

Hence, I appeared rather 'excitable' and even a little frustrated. That is a fair description of how I see my life looking back, you see, for as long as I can remember, I have worn a highly prickly habit; that is to say, my moods have been up and down, in response to life. No one knew what mood I'd be in from one day to the next and I guess that made it difficult for my Mum in particular, but also for others too!

I responded often unfavourably, to criticism and judgment. Many people might say, "Rightly so!" However, it never felt good to live this way. I was never happy, by snapping at someone.

Often, largely because of the Bronchitis/Asthma I had suffered with since I was 11, I was exonerated; my family wanted me to be well, and as the attacks seemed to coincide with an emotional outburst, they 'allowed' me to be 'lippy' and mostly get away with it.

In hindsight, I was probably a little spoilt because of my poor health. Bouts of Tonsillitis culminating in surgery to remove my tonsils, preceded the frightening lung condition, which then dominated my life through 4 decades!

I was a bit of a misfit growing up. I had few real friends and never really managed to 'belong', even though at 17 I found a whole tribe of other misfits in the 1970's & 80's Rock'n'Roll scene. I was shy with low self-esteem and felt different. I tried to fit in but a part of me held back. Yes, it was fun and oh how adventurous I felt when I spent weekends away with my tribe listening and dancing to the only music I've truly ever loved. Yet I felt straight-laced and boring next to everyone else. I couldn't seem to blend in. I knew so many people – still do – but something was missing.

At 25 I married and became a home-owner – largely to 'fit-in' and 'belong' doing the normal thing but later divorcing – we just weren't a good fit after all.

Another sub-culture became 'home' for me in my 30's when I discovered Rap, Hip Hop and New Jack Swing. I learned how to dress and dance to blend in and stand out at the same time! I listened to angry music and moved in angry circles. I began to adopt a different air – one that gave me confidence, and at the same time exuded 'attitude'! Yet still, something was missing! I'd be 'hard' on the outside, but inside, I was hurting. No one really knew me, nor spent much time trying to find out! I was still very much alone and getting used to it!

I started to have regular out-of-body experiences. The only way I can describe this is that whilst totally awake, I would step 'out of me' and look at me, marveling that I was treading the earth, in a physical body with the ability to have thoughts and knowing they were mine!

How could I share this with anyone? They'd think I was mad! So I kept it to myself, feeling even more removed from the crazy world in which I lived.

I met someone online after being single for a number of years and felt loved. Really loved for the first time. I began to feel joy and a sense of belonging. However, a full-blown connection was lacking. I stayed longer than I ought, feeling guilty that his love wasn't returned. My self-esteem plummeted; why couldn't I find me?!

When my lovely Daddy died in December 2004 just after my Mum's 70th birthday, I was distraught. In my grief, my prickliness turned to outrageous anger and I adopted an even darker shadow, than my former self. I was still nice much of the time, but being naughty was what people remembered me for. Santa was never going to pop by at this rate! ☺ Ho-Ho-No!

The worst thing about this dysfunction that had taken me over, was that there was no reason to behave this way. Simple as that, but it didn't stop me from continuing. Yes, I was hurting; truly hurting, and yet grief was not enough to show my pain. I had to take it further – for more than 2 years! I spiraled often out of control, crying with an intolerable pain in my heart, not knowing what to do!

The more upset I felt, the angrier I became. Not a pretty sight – ever!

Then in 2007, I discovered Tony Robbins followed by the magical Louise Hay, and the ever-so-calming Wayne Dyer. My shelf became laden with books all providing techniques to unleash my power, manage my anger and adopt an air of calm. After years of feeling angry, alone and helpless, I realised that the part of me that was missing had come alive! I felt like I was beginning to find my way and that people did actually like me – for me!

One part of my life however, had to end. It was well overdue and had been planned for a few months. Yet it didn't actually pan out, as in the meantime, someone new attracted my attention. What felt so right then – and still does – took my breath away, filled me with an intense passion I've never before experienced and I realised that for the first time, I was truly, madly and deeply 'In Love'.

There was a sudden shift, an all-change as it were, and I was heading on a new and vibrant path. And you know, this new feeling was both a blessing and a curse as a new body became evident; the green-eyed monster! The 'mad' part about being in love for me, was a feeling that I was 'not good enough' and I would therefore lose him! As a result, I became depressed and dysfunctional.

I know looking back, that I was so unprepared for love, not understanding exactly what it was nor how it would feel, that I was unworthy of it. It was like a lightening bolt repeating itself, every time I woke or set eyes on him. It was magic and yet so painful to my heart, as if it was breaking. Well yes, indeed it was; the hard shell I had protected it with, was cracking – and I was cracking up with it!

The shameful part of this new experience, was not that I didn't deserve it, but that I didn't realise I was being blessed. Every feeling I had ever felt in my entire angry life was illuminated! It was now that the lessons would be learned; now, that I would be shown the way to change. Now, that I stood to lose what I treasured the most! Love.

I cannot deny that my anger has stood between us like the proverbial elephant in the room! It is my lesson to learn and my lot to lose if not. And you know, through all of this, I have begun to find the real me and to love her. Phew, I didn't know I didn't love me! How blinded could I be? Not loving me meant I could not truly love another. The deep love I now feel is testament to that!

So what happened to the anger? Well, I cannot deny it's still a small part of me that appears when I am squeezed, however the change was understanding where anger belonged and where it didn't. (Just like me!)

I was listening to Wayne Dyer one day and it happened; you know, the lightbulb that flashes off in your head, the penny dropping, coupled with an epiphany! I realised I was often taking offense at the slightest thing. Taking offense?! Wow! Well that just took the biscuit! I was gobsmacked! Know why? Because I had been receiving this message for years, and I mean years!!!

I just didn't realise that I was offended by some things people had said to me. It's not that they were really hurtful, it's just that they didn't sit with my values! I didn't feel aligned with what they were saying, however there was no need to react in the way I often did! Many times it was simply none of my business!

As a storyteller for many years, I often built a story around something that had happened or was happening. But it wasn't always a happy story. I didn't see the truth, I saw what I had created. Often this was so far removed from the truth, it was pathetic!

I needed to learn from this and sought a teacher in Mike Fisher from the British Association of Anger Management, who within a weekly workshop setting, provided a set of tools to understand how to put anger in perspective. I then went on to learn about Compassion from Dr Chris Irons and Dr Charlie Heriot-Maitland of the Balanced Minds team at Kings College, London. I was becoming calmer and more eloquent in my conversations, rather than frustrated, argumentative and loud. I gave the stories in my head a different twist; I applied logic and emotional intelligence. I removed all untruths!

Mindfulness and compassionate mind training became a big part of my life and I began following the Emotional Intelligence (EI) work and strategies published by Daniel Goleman. My own Facebook group for EI became a source of dispersing my knowledge and gave me a sense of pride and worthiness that I was finally beginning to find my way.

What I feel people tend not to realise, is that anger in and of itself is unsightly and disturbing when extreme. Yet it is nevertheless, the effect of a cause that resides within us, often so deep as to never locate and remedy it.

I am not condoning anger and I wish I had never shown such extremes, however it has eventually taught me one thing. If I truly love myself, for what I do and how I think, I will not be angry. I will be complete and whole, without the need for anything nor anyone, to 'make me' feel loved.

As a continuing work in progress, I am on the road to identifying myself as truly compassionate toward myself and my fellow man and woman. I look to my inner child, my inner being and I love her for what she has accomplished and what she has yet to accomplish.

Life is a journey without a real destination other than death. Along this journey lies many challenges, much joy and often incredible pain. But what if we used these experiences as milestones to learn about ourselves, instead of being fixated on 'being right' to the point where anger descends on us? Hmmmmmm....now there's a thought!

I have realised many things over the past decade alone, and as a result I have changed my whole approach to life. Here are a few tips of my own to guide you to find your own:

- ❖ When I am tired, I rest and recoup. To resist may expedite feelings of lack, paranoia and overwhelm.
- ❖ When I am experiencing jealousy, I ask myself if the story I am creating is real. If it is not, there is no need to respond. I let it go.
- ❖ When I hear that someone has made a decision about me that I don't feel is true, it is none of my business, it is only their story and therefore there is no need to take offence.
- ❖ When someone is angry or frustrated, it is not up to me to buy into it nor get angry for or with them. It is definitely an opportunity for me to feel compassion for their plight.
- ❖ When I meet someone who is depressed, there is always something I can say about their life to inspire them. I will always give them my time and help them to see even a small chink of light. It's often all we need!

Where I find I'm speaking to someone who has lost a loved one, I often share my story of how my Dad is still with me, guiding me as he has from beyond my sight, to make a new set of choices that has created a life worth living. Yes, it hurts to lose a love, and yet love is a constant feeling which never dies, hence to feel it within us, means that it doesn't matter if it is not outside of us. We have enough! My blessings to you and yours in finding and enjoying your way through life and love. It's truly magical you know!

WALKING WITH THE SPIRIT WORLD...
BE THE BEST VERSION OF YOU
By
Mitch Garlington

Who am I?
You might know me as Mitch Garlington - Spiritual Medium - Psychic - Tarot Reader, and this is my story.

Like so many light workers we often have to experience pain and darker times before we can truly embrace the light within.

This is no different for men or women. We are all equal however our own input into this world grows and shapes us. Our actions set us apart, and ultimately we shape and become what we want to be.

Growing up as a child was both good and bad. I was blessed with a beautiful family that love me (and still do) unconditionally. However, unconditional love isn't always perfect, and can come with a cost.

From a very young age people seemed to know what was best for me and what I should be doing. This tended to be the trend with family, teachers, and even later in life with co-workers!

Everyone always seemed to know what I should be doing. Yet no one had taken the time to ask me what I wanted to do. This started with my Dad. I love him dearly, but it hasn't always been an easy road. From as far back as I can remember I was creative, mystical, an old soul on young shoulders.

I had always been made aware of the spirit world; it didn't scare me. I thought it was normal. It was only as I grew older I realised it wasn't 'correct' to be seeing these spirits and talking to them, so I quickly stopped talking about it, and kept it to myself.

While my creativity continued to flourish, my Dad I feel, felt he had failed as a parent; of course this was not true. I suppose when families bring children into the world, they have ideas and hopes and desires on how they will be and what they will do. My Dad had visions of us playing football together, going to matches and doing all things sports related. However, it was quickly apparent that was not going to be the case. I have never been into sport it bores the hell out of me. I see it as a way to fuel ego, greed and material wealth. I don't understand how a footballer can be paid ridiculous amounts of money to kick a ball up and down a field, whilst doctors and nurses save lives daily, yet are on (in some cases) minimum wage. But hey that's another story (don't get me started).

Through my Dad's own fear, he became a man on a mission to bring out the sportsman in me. All this did was cause confusion and made me feel less than correct. Was it so unnatural to not be into sport? For my Dad it certainly seemed like it was the end of the world, and I was pretty much written off as a lost cause thereafter. He will probably never realise how his own desires made me feel like I wasn't a normal boy.

Dad's demands backfired big time and if anything made my creativity flourish even more. Like a lot of creatives, when we are put in situations that make us feel uncomfortable, we use that as a fuel or energy to push forward.

From around the age of 7 or 8 my Witchyness kicked in. People around me laughed and mocked. They didn't get it or understand. The problem was I didn't care if they got it. What was there to get? I was a Witch end of!

People have different opinions on this subject and I can only speak from my own experience. Witchcraft for me is part of who I am, you are born with it. You don't choose to be a Witch. You feel it within you; it's part of the essence of who you are. This quickly became another taboo that was deemed unacceptable.

My Dad didn't get it or understand it, so therefore he felt I had no business being involved with it. Teachers and friends didn't get it either. The only person that truly supported me without question was Mum.

To her, a Mother's love meant true unconditionally love. If I was a Witch she was ok with that. She even made me a cape and hat much to my Dad's horror. She has always encouraged us to do what makes us happy, and be the best version of our self.

School and college days were very dark times. I was verbally bullied daily, from the start of the school day until home time. Lunch times would be spent alone, circling and walking the school playground.

I continued having secret conversations with the spirit world. It wasn't all the time it seemed to be in stages. Usually the pattern was if things where becoming even more difficult or harder than before, messages where given. Of course now I know it was my loved ones and spirit guides helping me, and pushing me forward. But I was very inexperienced and naïve back then.

Bomb shell number 3 was about to be dropped with some force. The elephant that was in the room had been building for a number of years; I was often called (by bullies and even my Dad on occasion) faggot, poofter, gay boy, etc

Be careful what you wish for...the time had come to let the world know I was indeed gay. Mum and my Sister kind of knew; it wasn't really a surprise when you would rather play with your Sister's dolls than go out with a ball! They were simply happy I was me and moved on. Dad however, thought my preferences were another personal attack on him. It was decided he wasn't to be told straight away.

My boyfriend who I was seeing was from London. He suggested I move in with him. I was only 16 so this was a big adventure to me; the big smoke and bright lights were calling. That's what I did and a few weeks later my Dad was given the news.

Being in London made it bearable, I wasn't around to have to listen to him belittling me. It's not that he is homophobic (or maybe on some level he is?) It's just that once again, he couldn't get his head around it.

So many questions! Was it something he had done? Had he failed as a parent? If I had eaten more greens, would that have stopped it? Just as it was with witchcraft, my own experience is that I have always been gay. It was never something I needed to discuss, I knew from about the age of 6 or 7.

You don't choose to full in love with the wrong sex, but if both parties are happy, and not causing any pain, the rest is nobody else's business!

Dad is one of those guys that really struggles with his own emotions; therefore for him, knocking something or someone, putting it or them down, is his way to cope. I was aware of this pattern from a young age, but also knew I needed to deflect that energy back. That was junk my Dad had to get his head around, and in no way was a reflection on me.

London helped at that period of time; it felt like true magic. I was able to explore all my true colours. I experienced 'the scene' and saw all walks of life; all shapes, sizes, genders and sexual orientations.

It was a place to escape the coldness of the human race, and just be around like-minded souls. No one was competing, everyone was free-spirited enjoying the music, dancing, singing, waving hands or a feather boa in the air.

For the first time in my life, even though I didn't know any of these people, I felt complete acceptance. Time is a good healer; by me not being around, Dad had the space he needed to make sense of the world, that had changed around him.

He called me up and wanted me to move back home as he had heard from Mum that I was struggling to get work due to lack of experience. He also added that if my boyfriend wanted to, he could also move back with me.

Complete shock was an understatement, as he had done a full U-turn. The magic of London was starting to drain me. I was homesick and missing nature. I think it was the best gift my Dad could have given me.

As a family we are all closer now than ever before. Whilst he will always 'do' my head in a little bit, I know in his own way that Dad does love me unconditionally, and he knows I love him; a true love between father and son that cannot be broken.

Years went by with my partner and I living a good life in Wiltshire; we had got our own rented flat together by this time. Life on the one hand was really good, but I was still having to justify what I was about.

Psychic Vampires started to appear from nowhere and without warning. I think when you're truly empathic, some people take advantage of your good nature. They see it as a skill they perhaps do not have and envy or want on some level.

Time after time my sexuality was brought up! Was I 100% gay? Had I done anything with a female? Questions after questions, that served no purpose.

Time moved on and I discovered I had to set boundaries. What I thought were relatively normal everyday jobs were becoming a real challenge. Not the work itself but the people within the work. I decided the time was right to fully embrace the mystic and magic within me.

The spirit world was poking me now more than ever; it was time to learn and understand how to fully connect, embrace and use these gifts I clearly had for the better.

I joined a development circle and kept this pretty quiet for the first few years. The bullying had seemed to continue from the school playground into adulthood. I questioned if it was more myself? Was I attracting this on some level? Often messages from loved ones would come through in meditation or other forms. Each time the same message was shown: "You are where you are meant to be!" One more hurdle? I struggled with this, I felt as though I was being brushed off and forgotten about in some way.

I became very tired... I was tired of having to justify who I was. If it wasn't my sexuality, it was what I was interested in, or how I spoke! There was always something. Months went by and I had a new manager at my place of work. By this time I was doing readings for people for free. I had also learned and had a great connection with Tarot. This new manager was Scottish and the most ignorant person I think I have worked with.

One day he was 'on at me' demanding certain jobs, that were actually for him to fulfil. I felt completely burnt out and had enough. He knew I was a medium but never questioned or talked about it. On this particular day, that was the subject of our conversation. He took great pleasure in trying to destroy my beliefs here. With that I felt the spirit of my Nan come in so close. A lot of family struggled with her, but we had a connection that was so strong both in life and death. She told me a test would be coming up, and that I would pass and I had to promise her to hand in my notice and follow my true calling if I was to be successful (which she made clear I would succeed).

Before I had time to digest the information, my manager asked me to bring someone through and prove this 'BS' was real. My instant reaction was to defend and deny his request, for this is not how the spirit world work.

However, once again, be careful what you ask for!

With that, several of his family members came forward. They showed me how he looked, names, dates, types of passing, personal accounts that he knew, and in some cases had never told anyone. He went outside pacing up and down the car park - it was like he had indeed seen a ghost.

He turned a shade of white and then grey with shock. He had received a big slap in the face. I looked in the doorway and saw my Nan once more. You have completed your task. You have stayed true to yourself, and you have the knowing and trust that the spirit world does not judge you, they work with you as they have always done. It is time now to be the best version of yourself.

With that I knew 100% I could create my own world, and walk daily with the spirit world. I resigned and set myself up as a self-employed spiritual medium. The rest is history as they say!

My main message to you is this: "Always be the best version of you. Pay close attention to the world around you, they might not get it nor understand but that's ok!"

At no point in my journey did I change or tweak the essence of who I was. I have always embraced my own power. People around me haven't always liked that, or felt threatened in some way. But that is their junk to deal with, not mine.

It's funny, as when someone becomes successful you suddenly find 'ghosts' from your past, coming to you wanting your help. The one-time bullies suddenly sought and needed advice and guidance. I was told by a mentor very early on: "You need to grow a thick skin, you are too nice, you will get spat out by the spiritual circles".

For anyone who is not aware of my journey, I have achieved with the backing of the spirit world, a lot in a short space of time.

I have never changed nor altered who I am to be accepted. Both in spiritual circles nor in everyday life. I have always stayed true to my sacred heart, and my higher inner soul. To change or alter who I am would be like putting a mask on.

I am simply 'Mitch'.

My message is – "Always be the best version of yourself. NEVER change this! If people have a problem, that's something that is rooted within them. Shine bright and sparkle like the true star and true light YOU possess within. Mother Earth is fighting to regain her beauty, but she cannot win alone. Continue to work from a place of love, as this is the platform that will allow the world we all share, to flourish and heal.

-End-

A JOURNEY THROUGH DEPRESSION
By
Anne Dickson

My journey through this often-debilitating illness has been both a curse and a blessing!

Many reading this last statement of depression being a blessing, will of course be wondering how an illness could possibly be a blessing! Well, I will outline briefly how I have come to this conclusion about my journey through depression.

I think it's most likely something I was predisposed to suffer from. It appears that it's genetic and has run through my family for generations.

At first, I was put on medication which often didn't agree with me. It seemed to make my symptoms worse; moods darker, crazy nightmares, a never-ending list of problems, with anxiety and a debilitating lack of self-worth thrown into the mix! I always questioned the use of medication and over the years fought hard to be on little or no medication at all.

20 Years on: I was made redundant from a job that I loved, but this too was a blessing, though it didn't feel like it at the time!

I had always wanted to study Aromatherapy but could never find the time! My new-found freedom of not working nine to five allowed me to go back to college to study. I really enjoyed the course and as a prerequisite of studying Aromatherapy, I needed to study Anatomy and Physiology and Swedish Massage. I loved learning all of this, and soon realised that essential oils could play a big part in my recovery from depression. I used the oils in blends and also used oils on their own to help elevate my mood.

After qualifying as an Aromatherapist I looked at learning Reflexology. I studied this at night school, as I was working as a chef during the day. I really enjoyed studying this and the relaxation from the treatments helped to calm me down and also helped to keep my mood elevated, and not rely so much on the medication I was taking to control my moods.

Both these therapies have helped me in overcoming depression. I am now on the lowest dose of conventional medication with a view to coming off it completely!

I have also qualified in Crystal Therapy and have been attuned to Reiki Master Level.

At the beginning of this short introduction I mentioned that depression was also a blessing! The blessing is I would never have studied Aromatherapy or Reflexology Crystal Therapy or become a Reiki practitioner had I not been looking for ways out of a depressive illness and found ways in which to help myself regain full health! I would also never have met all the people I met on my journey through self-healing.

My advice to anyone reading this would be, always look for other ways to help heal you, whether it be mental, emotional or physical illnesses. Nature has given us everything we need, it's just a matter of tapping into and finding out all of Mother Earth's natural resources.

-End-

BACK FOR GOOD
By
Donna B

A journey of fifty years
began in nineteen-sixty-seven
I was four years old
when I knew of my connection to heaven.

Some memories as sharp as a knife
some faded
Many dreams and aspirations
soon became jaded.

Opinions, beliefs, religion,
control, rules and more
Stunted, dulled excitement,
knocked creativity for sure.

I loved bonfire night,
loud noises, colour, smells, fire
Plenty of ammunition
for art in school it did inspire.

Troubled childhood,
growing up mostly unseen
Hidden, except from Nan,
who became my queen.

We would bake cakes, make faggots,
eat crusts of hot bread,
We'd watch TV, read books, play cards
and have biscuits before bed.
Freedom came in the form of a season ticket
for the local pool
School holidays floating, swimming, diving, acting and playing the
fool.

One session ran into another
many hours I would spend
No surprise my Sun sign is Pisces,
and water my bestest friend.

Before too long I was an adult
who just tried to survive
Taking risks, breaking rules,
most all events contrived.

Living in a body of betrayal,
let down in my very own World,
A lifetime of experiences
in a short space continually unfurled.

I sit here at just fifty-four years young,
wiser mid journey of life
With no children, diabetes, polycystic ovaries
and I'm a second-time wife.

Discovering my Purpose
I now see as an adventure,
Gratitude I have plenty
especially with no dentures.

I have finally found me,
the very essence of who I am,
Seeing again for the first time
as a babe once in a pram.

Though no question about it,
it was always written in the sky,
Now growing with astrology,
I get it, I totally understand why.

The rule breaking Aquarius,
positioned at birth as my ascendant,
My chart screaming psychic medium
as I wear my Moldavite pendant.

Born to share,
to support, to lead, to teach,
Goals there are plenty
but none out of reach.

Stronger, supported, wiser
and working through the still many fears,
Soon to be exposed by the movement
of planet Jupiter in two years.

Now to get used to being hidden no more,
living a life I should,
With love in my heart and a song in my head
"I Am Back For Good"

Coming soon...
'Conscience Writes'

Donna B.

-End-

"Do not hide your grief. Your loss has transformed you;
it has given you a
purpose and a voice.

Do not be silent."

Cath B

THE NAME OF THE ROSE
By
Wendy Salmon

The rose has a secret
Ask it for its name
Its scent hides many favours
And will not take the blame.

Soft are its petals
Sharp are its thorns
Be careful how to handle it
And be careful not to scorn.

For within lies its secret
so soft, so loving, so fair
Be at one and the same with the name of the rose
And ask it not to stare.

Ever since there has been blooms of roses opening to the life-raising sun, there has been beauty, wonder and love.

Yes, the secret of life lies in all the wonderous stages of seed, cutting, roots, shoots and flowering, as in the secrets of our bountiful evolution, where we were once the seed in embryonic form, full of potential and miracles. Then the cutting when separated from the safety of our mother`s wombs, blossoming into the roots of childhood where we learned how to be, how to do and how to grow.

Then into the shoots of youth, exploring, experimenting and trying to find our place in our view of an uncertain world which we learn can be cruel yet also beautiful and awash with possibilities.

Before flowering, comes the bud, where we find our potential and route through the various roads and mountains we must traverse if we want to grow and expand into the vastness of being.

Oh and finally there, the flowering, growing into all of the seasons in segments of change and time into the most awesome beauty of ourselves which bestows mountainous gifts to this world in the form of each and every one of us that opens to the secret of the rose.

We are who we are and although transgressions do have to be held accountable for, we are ultimately destined to be who we came here to be and need not feel guilty nor ashamed to be this wonderous soul standing before creation in honesty, decency and truth.

We can be soft, we can be sharp as thorns, but always, ultimately the expression of a life lived and loved into the flower that is us trying to find its platform – it`s showing.

So, beating yourself cruelly for actions taken in pain and fear need not mar your character, as chastising the rose for its thorns will keep it from becoming a rose when exposed to acceptance and the mirrors of self-care.

The rose is the expression of who we are; this is our secret, this is our life and this is our name – and our name is LOVE.

Love and blessings,
Wendy Salmon

-End-

A JOURNEY OF COMPASSION
By
Linda Sands

I was a small girl of 7 when my mother left. I was bewildered by the anger, the sadness and then the hostility.

There was no more nurturing and feeling small - I was now 'the woman of the house' and learned to cook and keep house.

That's what I knew - that's what I began to believe as love, to be worthy, to be loved; by deeds and acts of kindness and thoughtfulness. Being told not to take people for granted, not to be selfish and not to be too big for your boots.

Those childhood lessons – oh how they would remain and become the reminder of a childhood without compassion.

There was no grieving for the loss of a Mother or the loss of a childhood. There was growing up to do and being brave.

The dreams of heroism and being admired.

The dream of being someone important. But soon a substitute Mother arrived and the big girl was relegated to second place.

No extra cuddles or sitting on Daddy's knee.

No time to grieve.

Soon the real adult world beckoned. I was different to the others, I didn't fit in. I didn't share the 'childish' humour - the child had long gone.

The adult world was confusing; it complicated the search for belonging and for love.

Within 54 years, three marriages were done and dusted. Love was still elusive with a deep profound emptiness.

The journey began; the search for knowing and understanding.

At last the little girl speaks. The little girl has found the love she has sought.

The love has been found in compassion - compassion and understanding of and within herself.

The journey continues.....

-End-

RETURNING TO ME!
By
Lizi May Davis

Even after years of doubt, and ups and downs, sometimes all it takes is one remark from a friend or family member, to trigger a response that will make you 100% adamant that things now need to change. Not just 'need' to change, but MUST change, in order for you to really start living the life you want.

For me, this remark came from my Brother. We were visiting our Dad's memorial oak tree; we tidied up the area and cleaned off the plaque, as usual. Then came the words, "You'll be the same age as Dad was soon".

To my brother's surprise I burst into tears, and I got the sense he felt bad for reminding me of this, but he just hugged me and reassured me like any brother would do.

I'll never forget this moment though, it was a massive turning point in what had become an increasingly lonely and unhappy life for me. You see I was in one of those relationships that, of course means a lot to you, but ultimately is not healthy or 'right' for either partner. And as time went on I felt more and more like a ghost in my own marriage.

I was approaching 35 years old, and I was reflecting upon the sad fact that my wonderful Dad had passed away from liver cancer at the young age of just 36.

It sounds silly I know, but from this point I almost felt like I only had until I reached the same age to really live my life, and a drive grew inside of me to make sure this happened, no matter what.

My husband had suggested I move back to London temporarily, while I began working on my dream business, and I decided this was a great idea. It gave me time and space by myself and I was also able to begin monthly mentoring with a wonderful lady, who will now forever remain a true friend.

At first the mentoring focused mainly on my business, but it became clear that, in order for my business to succeed, I would have to work on other areas of my life too, as any negativity I was experiencing elsewhere would ripple out into every other area of my being.

This was a revelation to me!

We're so good at segmenting everything and just getting on with what we have to do until we can switch off from it later on, and I began to realise that any time my Husband and I spent apart was acting like a Band-Aid and giving things a chance to settle down before we spent time together again and the tension and loneliness for me – possibly him as well – would creep back in.

I could ignore this no longer, and so, as well as working on my inner self, I began to also work on setting intentions for the type of relationship I really wanted for myself. I knew this would either shift my marriage into a more positive state or it would end it altogether, because I had faith that the Universe would bring me what I was asking for.

As the time for me to return to my Husband drew closer, a huge knot of dread grew and grew in my stomach. I ultimately took this as a sign that I should not leave London to go back to him, and though it was an extremely tough decision and many tears were shed, I know now that I was right to listen to this gut feeling.

We began distance counselling - good old Google Hangouts – and I increased my mentoring from monthly to weekly sessions. I also began to focus more on meditation, journaling and spending more time with my friends and family.

As the year progressed I began to feel more and more like my old self – someone I hadn't quite realised had been withdrawn for so many years, even before meeting my husband. And all of a sudden I found my voice again; my intuition was on fire and I noticed more feelings of peace and contentment.

I believe this comes from being true to yourself.

In getting to this point, some of the more noticeable 'shifts' for me came after receiving so much encouragement and support from the wonderful souls of the Discover Your Purpose Facebook group (set up by my mentor, Sam) after I had gone 'Live' to talk to them about my marriage counselling and the journaling our counsellor wanted me to do around my Dad's death. I wasn't sure where to begin in journaling about this, but their advice allowed me to let the words flow and after reading it out in our counselling session the next week, I felt a lightness about me and a wonderful sense of relief.

Funnily enough, I'm not sure it helped my Husband to understand me any better, but it most definitely helped me see myself and everything I wanted much more clearly!

Another big shift came for me after a mentoring session during which Sam guided me through a Womb healing.

I have to say I had initially been a little sceptical about this, but I remained open minded as I so wanted to keep working on, and improving myself, as much as possible!

I was blown away by what came up for me during this session and I immediately felt 'different' for having done it. I can't quite explain how, except that there was an overwhelming feeling of positivity and a sense that everything was going to be OK.

It wasn't even a week after this session that I just woke up one day and *knew* that now was the right time for my Husband and I to let each other go.

Before speaking with him I wrote down how I wanted the conversation to go and the boundaries I would keep for myself throughout. I was pleasantly surprised by how amicably it went, and though I know both of us felt some sadness, I think we also both understood that it was for the best.

Remember I mentioned that I had set intentions for the relationship I really wanted? Well, completely unexpectedly, the most wonderful man appeared in my life! And he's everything I had purposefully intended, and more. Had my husband and I kept 'trying' there would have been no space in my life for this to happen at all!

My business is also shifting.

From experiencing all I've been through this year, and talking to other women about similar situations, I've realised just how many people lose themselves in unhappy relationships, and with this loss of self will also come a lack in confidence.

This has lit a huge fire in me to be able to use my coaching skills to help newly single women come back to themselves, regain their confidence, and live the life they truly want and deserve.

When I think back to this time last year, there's no possible way I could have imagined I'd be where I am now, and it goes to show that sometimes it really is *so* important to say, "Enough is enough" and put yourself first, because if you're not living the life you want to live, how can you be all you want to be to the people closest to you as well?! ☺

Thank-you so much for reading my story, I hope it provides some sort of hope or inspiration.

-End-

THE REMEMBRANCE OF THE SOUL
By
Tamlyn Jayne Wolfenden

Each soul is born into this life perfect, whole and complete and is a fully connected being to their soul.

As the soul grows, environmental conditioning and society expectations wear away at this connection and start to disconnect the body from the soul. This results in the person disconnecting to their knowingness, abandoning their wisdom and they then begin to view the world from outside of themselves rather than the focus coming from within.

The soul never loses hope and continues to whisper from deep within, for it knows that one day there will be a remembrance and one day they will both be reunited.

Time passes and the person becomes lost in daily life. Worry replaces trust, sadness replaces joy and the yearning for a connection causes the constant seeking for betterment and a pressure on relationships with other people.

The disconnected person believes that if only they find a special someone will they feel the connection they vaguely remember.

They believe that this is when they will feel happiness and feel complete.

Then there comes a point where one day the suffering and anxiety becomes too much, the competition and striving grows too tiring and the busyness and distraction of life become less appealing.

There comes a point where there is nowhere outside left to search and so the person, as they crumble, desperate and feeling alone, is then forced to look within.

There in the darkness of unknowingness, the silent whispers of the soul grow stronger. There in the void of nothingness, something unique begins to emerge.

It is when there is nothing left but faith and when one must surrender, it is here that Soul Remembrance is awakened and the uniting process begins.

It is here that inner wisdom is discovered, inner vision is deactivated and life takes on a whole new meaning.

It is in this moment that the inner fire is ignited and the connection is reborn.

It is from this day forward you have a knowing of your soul purpose and acceptance of your path for now you dance in perfect harmony with your soul.

-End-

THE MISSING PIECE
By
Vicki Briant

Have you ever begun the process of building a beautiful jigsaw puzzle only to realise a tiny piece is missing?

The Missing Piece is an extremely accurate description of my infertility journey; this short story details how I rose from the depths of despair, to living an extraordinarily, fulfilling and satisfying life. It is a tale of the pursuit for my missing jigsaw puzzle piece, and how divine intervention changed the course of my life.

I had been aware of my missing piece for some time; initially I felt nothing more than slight frustration. You see, my puzzle was coming along beautifully; I felt sure that my missing piece would make an appearance at any moment. I was building a masterpiece with such ease and elegance. Every single piece was interlocking so smoothly and snuggly to reveal a very happy life. This was a puzzle that was a joy to build and there had been no difficulties thus far.

The pieces of the puzzle were adorned with delightful images. The bottom left hand corner displayed a romantic love story, and as more tiny pieces were positioned in the puzzle, it revealed many more beautiful images. An emigration to Spain, a wonderful life in the sunshine, a majestic fairy-tale wedding in Greece, so many exciting and gleeful pieces were carefully positioned to create a blissful picture. There was just one more very important piece, that would really make this puzzle the masterpiece envisioned.

It was in June 2013 that the initial frustration for the missing piece elevated to another level, fear and panic slipped into the place where frustration had resided for so long. This is when everything changed, the time had now come to launch the search party for the missing piece.

The pursuit of the missing piece led us to a fertility clinic for some tests.

The devastating news we received that fateful day, quickly led us to a place where the missing piece was fast becoming an elusive piece. We were told that I had premature ovarian failure. A simple definition of the rather depressing diagnosis is that my basket of eggs was accelerating to empty at an incredibly hasty speed. I was told that proceeding to IVF with my own eggs posed a less than 3% chance of success. It was suggested that our best possible option would be to use donor eggs. This was an incredibly difficult decision to make and there were many factors to consider.

My heart ended up ruling in the decision-making process, my head knew that our best option was donor egg, however, how could I not try with my own eggs? Surely this would work for us.

Just a couple of months later we were amid our first IVF treatment. This was a relatively short-lived process and one that came to a devastatingly premature end. The day of egg retrieval is where I lost all hope, a day when my life changed forever. There were no eggs. The puzzle piece I had been searching for, had been snatched away from my grasp. I'm not sure there are any words that could adequately describe the pain that I felt that day. My heart broke into so many pieces, not only for myself but for my Husband and family also.

How had this happened? My puzzle had been so easy to build up to this point, why was it now so hard to complete my masterpiece? These questions amongst others were the start of what felt like falling into a black hole, and having absolutely no escape. There were no answers, and this led me into a very deep and extremely dark place of depression. At this point my only available options in moving forward were donor egg IVF or adoption, both very personal choices and ones that would take some time to consider. I needed time to grieve the biological children I would never have, before I could even contemplate such decisions.

Life seemed to somehow just linger in limbo for a couple of years. The doctor prescribed me anti-depressants and I decided to take them even though I had always been against medication of this kind.

I needed the pain to stop and the medication proved useful in aiding my recovery, even if it was just numbing the sharp pain. The medication somehow enabled me to step back and process all that had happened.

The decision of using donor eggs was not one that came easy to me, and I chose not to proceed in this way. It's an extremely personal decision for a woman to make and I bare no judgement on anyone that has chosen this path in life. It just wasn't the right choice for me and as painful as that decision was to make, it was important that I remained true to myself.

The other option of adoption was a huge consideration for us and one that we were very open to, however living outside of the UK proved to be a large stumbling block in the process, and we again decided not to proceed in this way. This was the hardest part in my journey, the realisation that the time had come to stop searching for the missing piece to my puzzle, one of the hardest decisions I have ever had the misfortune in making. Everything I had planned for my life from a young age had now been ripped away from me. I now had to come to terms with the heart-rending fact that I would not become a Mother.

As the weeks and months continued to slowly drift past, I was desperate to find the joy and happiness that had been so prevalent in my life before this ordeal had begun. There was a humungous void in my life and I wanted the old ME back. The happy, young woman full of hope that seemed to have been lost back in the recovery room at the non-egg retrieval, was fighting to find a way back into this world. I prayed and pleaded to my Angels, "Please help me move forward; please show me the way". Not long after my plea for help, my beautiful Angels answered my prayers.

It was just another boring day at work as a dental receptionist, when a stranger entered my life and changed the course of my future. He was most definitely sent by my Angels; divine intervention in the form of inspiration.

As the gentleman waited for his dental appointment he began talking to me about his life. His exciting and adventurous tales inspired me immensely, I felt something I hadn't felt for an incredibly long time. I felt hope again, as I listened intently to how he had travelled the world by boat and motorhome; it pricked every fibre of my being with excitement and enthusiasm for life again.

Here was the answer from my Angels; inspired messages from a stranger. My Angels were giving me an opportunity to create a new piece to my puzzle. An incredible way to move forward.

I'm extremely happy to report that I listened to my Angels that day and created a whole new life for my Husband, dog and I. We now travel Europe in a motorhome every fortnight. The day the Angels showed me hope again, was the day my healing journey began. Since we embarked on our new adventure in February 2017, I have continued my healing path in various ways. I've worked with several coaches and embarked on various programmes that have all played a huge part in aiding my healing. I now find joy and happiness in the simple things in life; I am now able to feel gratitude for this incredible journey.

My masterpiece today looks very different to the one that I had envisioned all those years ago. Just like life, our puzzles may not always pan out the way we had originally planned. However, there is always an opportunity to create a new piece. I am living proof that it is possible to find happiness, joy and fulfilment when you create a new piece to your puzzle.

I am currently writing a book about my journey, with more in-depth detail, due to be published in 2018. If you would like to be notified of the publication date you can opt in via my website. I also run a support group on Facebook for women who may be experiencing or have experienced a similar journey to myself.

If you would like to follow us on our journey around Europe, please feel free to use my links on the Resources page.

-End-

DISCOVERING MY PURPOSE
By
Jo Gomme

I was asked for my story
And so I sat down,
with a pen and paper
all scattered around.

The thoughts in my head
were all jumbled about,
nothing made sense
no words were profound.

And then I remembered
whilst I was a child,
there were things that I knew
that I hadn't been told!

These things, these thoughts,
they appeared in my head,
but when I spoke them out loud
"Don't be silly" she said.

For Mum didn't know
these things that I knew,
like Granny turning up
just out of the blue!

"I told you" I said
"I told you she would",
"Don't be silly" you said
"It does you no good."

So after a while
I used to keep quiet,
and these things that I knew
soon all fell silent.

As years went by
and as I grew,
there was an uncertain feeling
that started to brew.

Eyes that would watch
but nobody was there,
voices would whisper
but I couldn't quite hear.

Witches and demons
interest me lots,
fairies and gnomes
all their stories and plots.

My parents thought that 'it's just a faze'
all the girls love to go through this craze,
but as I got older, my interests grew
the magic, the witchcraft and the crystals I knew.

My interest in energy
was sparked in a way,
that I never forgot
As Grandad passed, one day.

That feeling I had
the knowing he had gone,
*** these were all felt   ***
before the phone call.

It happened again
with an Aunt of mine,
and then again,
with Nanny this time.

I was starting to feel cursed
as my other Grandad passed,
yet somehow I knew
that all was not lost.

I began in earnest
remembering my gifts,
and learning new ways
to tap into it.

Crystals have power,
they sing and vibrate.
Reiki is subtle,
gentle yet great.

Then came Silver Spheres,
from the great Moira Bush,
she taught me so much
about energy and the source.

Colour Mirrors was next,
founded by Melissie Jolly,
I could use colour to heal,
what a fabulous modality!

Since learning these tools
I have uncovered a lot,
I've cleared out my past
and know now what I forgot.

Past lives have been honoured
Ancestors forgiven,
Soul Contracts are noted,
they are there for a reason.

I have had my fair share
of stresses and strains,
and although it's been hard
I'm coming out of the rain.

The dark gloom is fading
by the light of the sun,
the biggest star in the sky
- that's where we are from.

We are all made of stardust
of energy and love,
and that is my path now
to make sure we all know.

To know we are energy
To know we are love,
To remember our home,
amongst the stars above

So if you would like
to know where you're from,
pop onto my website
at jogomme.com

-End-

LOSS & ANXIETY LED ME TO MY PURPOSE
By
Rachel Pernak-Brennon

I woke up in the middle of the night with this unbelievable heaviness in my chest. I remember grasping my hand to my chest, I could hardly get my breath out. I felt like I was suffocating – the hole for my throat was getting narrower and narrower with each raspy breath. I grabbed my partner and said through gasps of no air, "I think......I'm having.....a heart... attack...I CAN'T......BREATH".

My wheezing was getting louder and louder, it was dark, cold, windy and I was dying. I was only 21.

This was my 1st experience of anxiety. I was 21 and had had one of the worst years of my life. My family had decided that my life choice to settle down rather than pursuing the opera career they had expected of me (I was classically trained in Italian Arias), was too much for them to accept so I had been cast out and told I was dead to them now, I had no family. My Mum had been my best friend as well as my Mum. Only being the 4 of us, we had kept a closeness and unbreakable bond; I trusted them all with my life.

I don't think they understood how painful it was to stand up on stage, singing with all eyes on you, listening. To literally bear your soul through your voice and the pressure of performing in such a competitively pressuring environment temporarily took all my love of music away. I remember my brother telling me that I was a disappointment and a failure as I had not lived up to their expectations of me. He then went on to suggest, "Do everyone a favour and wrap your car round a tree somewhere". So, I no longer had a blood family and this was my 1st major experience of anxiety caused through loss.

My partner encouraged me to sit up and just breathe slowly and deeply, I was urging him to call an ambulance but I think it was no surprise to him, seeing how deeply and utterly low I had been over that year and this was how it had eventually shown itself in my body.

Incidentally, I later discovered my Mum had not wanted this situation at all, but that the pressure from my domineering Father and Brother had been too much for her to deal with, so we ended up having secret phone calls and messages until 20 years later when my Mum made my Dad drive her to my house as I had given birth to twins and she knew I needed her. (We always had an unbreakable bond and connection, so this did not surprise me although seeing them on the doorstep did at the time!!)

This was my 1st massive experience of loss. Loss comes in many forms, loss through death, loss of good friends, loss of treasured objects and loss through estrangement as was my situation here. All can bring on Anxiety - and in my case, Asthma, IBS and other subsequent issues too.

I will talk later about Oils and how they helped my Anxiety-induced health issues, but a wonderful oil to use for loss involving grief is Frankincense. My recipe for this is in the next section.

The day following my anxiety attack, I went to see my GP as I was still wheezing, and sure enough, I had underlying asthma which the anxiety had brought out. I had never experienced asthma before but according to research from Asthma UK, even mild asthma can be brought about by an anxiety attack.

I tried to discuss my emotions but sadly I left armed with steroid inhalers; 1 for preventing an attack and 1 for easing an attack if the preventer didn't work effectively as well, and an appointment in a few weeks.

At my next appointment, peak flow tests were carried out and I was termed Asthmatic on my records and given more medication. I decided I was not going to continue being given more and more medication* – I decided to look at treating the onset of my anxiety-induced asthma attack.

Please note that I am not suggesting you stop using your medication, but to look into why you have got Asthma and work on that.

Stress and Anxiety Attacks

So, my year of unbearable sadness had erupted into a full-blown anxiety attack, sometimes known as a Panic Attack. My body had become overwhelmed with ongoing stress.

When your body is under stress, it stimulates the nervous system to do its thing. It is important to note that stress is a part of life, but how we deal with stress is what causes the problems if it is not managed.

It is also important for me to say here that through my years of study, I now know that most physical illnesses can be related to an emotional issue, and in my case, the lungs are related to grief and loss, so it is no surprise that my emotional upset surrounding losing my blood family showed itself in my lungs as asthma and anxiety panic attacks.

I hope that by sharing the physiological workings of stress, that you might understand the relevance of carrying out the coping techniques I used, and how to teach to others, to help them deal with their stress and anxiety too.

You will soon see how amazing our bodies are at naturally dealing with stress and anxiety. Most of these initial survival functions are caused by the body secreting Adrenalin and Cortisol.

It is the Adrenalin that gives your body this surge of energy to fight or flee from the threat, by increasing your heart rate, your energy supplies and your heightened awareness of everything around you.

Cortisol helps your body use sugar (glucose from your bloodstream) and fat energy stores from your liver, as stress responses to help your body with a Fight or Flight response.

The Nervous System has 2 parts – The Sympathetic and the Parasympathetic and the related symptoms are tabled below.

Sympathetic Nervous System	Parasympathetic Nervous System
Recognises a threat and prepares the body to deal with that threat by either Fight or Flight.	Relaxes the body and slows down the heightened intensity of all the functions that the Sympathetic Nervous System had caused
Increases Heart Rate Increases Blood Pressure Dilates Pupils Increases Oxygen from middle of body to the extremities (running away is more important than digesting food in a threatening situation!) Inhibits flow of Saliva in mouth	Slows down Heart Rate Lowers Blood Pressure Contracts Pupils Returns normal oxygen flow to whole of body improving digestion of food etc Returns flow of Saliva in mouth
Inhibits bladder function	Normalises bladder function
Metabolic rate increases	Metabolic rate returns to normal

Once the threat has been dealt with, the body's Parasympathetic Nervous System kicks in and returns everything back to our normal functioning level; the heart rate slows down, digestive system behaves more normally, oxygen flows more evenly within the body, pupils contract in our eyes and we generally calm down.

Without turning this into an anatomy and physiology lesson you can see how effective the Sympathetic Nervous System is at preparing our bodies for stress but also how important it is that our Parasympathetic Nervous System kicks in to calm everything back down.

When our bodies become more and more stressed, therein lies the imbalance and that is when our problems can arise. The more stress we experience over a period of time, the more our bodies are going to be in a constant state of stress. Our mind also kicks in, we feel more and more out of control, and we become so used to this heightened level of stress that it becomes normal for us to feel threatened by situations. When our mind starts finding the ongoing stress overwhelming, becoming significant enough to interfere in our daily life, this is Anxiety.

Our mind tries to prepare us for the impending stresses to our bodies in various different ways, resulting in the different varieties of anxiety: OCD, GAD, PTSD, and Depression to name but a few. I was eventually diagnosed with Anxiety, Asthma, Depression & IBS.

Unless the cycle is broken, we will eventually break too. So, what did I do that helped me?

My Magical Introduction to Precious Oils

I adore essential oils, so I initially revisited an old book my Mum had given me about Aromatherapy. I had first been introduced to the wonders of precious oils when my Mum and I had gone along to a WI talk at our village hall in Newport, Saffron Walden. I was 13 years old. The talk was delivered by this amazing lady called Teddy Fearnhamm. Following the talk, we were invited to create our own blend to bathe in that night.

Oh My Word! I remember feeling a knowing whilst I was mixing my blend, almost like I had done it before. Like some kind of Witch mixing a potion!! A few days later my Mum took me along to Teddy's house in the village as my Mum suffered with blood pressure and had asked Teddy for a consultation and something to help. We walked into this aroma filled house of magical glass bottles and jars, and I just filled with excitement, awe and wonder. Teddy's potion helped my Mum, and we became avid users of oils after this.

So, I opened that book and filled my mind with as much info as I could on how different oils helped anxiety and the conditions my anxiety was creating. I made up the recipes and I started to feel more in control. Then I started experimenting with my own recipe blends, so I could wear the blends as a perfume instead, enabling me to feel treated all through the day.

This led me to enroll on courses and in 1997, 4 years after my first anxiety attack, I opened a little Apothecary shop where I would make and sell all my creations. My Mum had managed to come down alone that weekend and helped me bottle my oils ready for the opening; it was during this lovely weekend that she reminded me of my Grandma's Recipe Book; it was then that I knew why it had all felt so familiar to me mixing oils and creating potions.

My Grandma (my Mum's Mum) lived in Lancashire, the North of England (not far from Pendle Hill). She had been a nurse in the war, and she was also a 'Wise Woman'. She sadly died before I had been born but many people used to say I was the spitting image of my Grandma. Apparently we both shared quite a unique little cough which would happen when feeling nervous!!!

So, my Grandma used to have premonitions (which both my Mum and I have), she also used to read tea-leaves, palms and make up herbal remedies. It was all done behind closed curtains, as 'in those days it wasn't the done thing'!! People would visit Lizzy (Elizabeth Cooke) for help with all manner of ailments and she would help. She wrote her cures and recipes in a large notebook which was a Lancashire baking recipe book from the front but if you turned it upside down and around to the back, all her cures and herbal recipes would be there. So, it is no surprise that it all felt so familiar to me – it was in my Maternal Blood.

All through my training, I learnt how precious essential oils work on healing, and through my intuition I created the most beautiful and effective blends which people now come back for time and time again.

Oils work by entering the bloodstream, either via inhaling through the nose or absorption through the pores in the skin by massaging. Oils also have links with emotions as many people associate certain memories to smell. I love Honeysuckle as it grew at the side of our garage when I was little. Smelling honeysuckle always gives me a happy calm feeling as it transports me back to being a carefree little girl. So very often, we can use a roller blend of oils that not only offer therapeutic benefits but also bring you happy memories to give you a sense of calmness.

Essential oils are therefore extremely powerful when it comes to healing both physical and emotional issues. Physically they work by entering the bloodstream and the chemical components work in exactly the same way as any type of medication, except these are extracted from plants, flowers and trees. As I have said, they are also excellent at helping with emotional issues as they work on the Limbic part of the Brain (the emotions and memories section) when inhaled via the Olfactory system.

An oil that I found really helped not only my emotional feelings of loss, my breathing but also my anxiety was **Frankincense**, also known as Boswellia Carteri. It is extracted from the resin of the Olibanum tree. It has a deeply meditative aroma and was famous for its embalming properties during Mummifications in Ancient Egypt, so is a natural preservative and can even be added to creams as an anti-aging treatment. Frankincense has helped me massively with my anxiety.

One of my favourite recipes for anxiety using Frankincense is:
✓ 30mls carrier oil such as Grapeseed Oil
✓ 4 drops Boswellia Carteri (Frankincense)
✓ 2 drops Cananga Oderata (Ylang-Ylang)
✓ 4 drops Lavendula Augustifolia (Lavender)
✓ Either 2 drops Arthemis Nobilis (Roman Chamomile) if evening
✓ Or 2 drops of Ravensara Aromatica (Ravensara) if morning

As I have already mentioned, Frankincense is excellent for anxiety and helping to encourage deeper breathing, add to this Ylang-Ylang which slows heart rates and blood pressure down, Lavender which is a famous de-stresser but also an anti-inflammatory so excellent for Asthma, and finally, either Roman Chamomile which has sedative-like properties so excellent for aiding sleep, or Ravensara, which is a similar aroma to Eucalyptus but is a much more gentle decongestant and suitable for children. This remedy is a go-to for helping to induce calmness, sleep and breathe better.

You can add 5mls of this blend to a filled bath of warm water and soak in it. To optimise the effects, you can then massage 5mls into your body just as you would a body lotion each evening. You will sleep so much better. You can also add a few drops of this blend to an oil burner or electric diffuser (you will need to add water to this also) or even pour some of the oil blend onto a tissue and gently inhale.

An anxious mind often affects sleep and I find that by making a blend of Ylang-Ylang, Roman Chamomile & Lavender in Grapeseed oil and massaging this onto the soles of the feet, I get to sleep far easier and wake up far more rested. I would recommend 5 drops of each in 30ml of the carrier oil Grapeseed.

Because anxiety is usually caused as a result of something else, I often create personal blends for individual needs and you can contact me via the contact details listed in this book if you would like to have a personal consultation and blend created for your individual concerns.

Anxiety & IBS

IBS is not in itself a condition so to speak but rather a diagnosis you are given when everything else has been ruled out. So, I had Anxiety induced IBS. I would panic at the thought of going somewhere new because I was worried in case I needed to rush to the loo, and wouldn't know where it was.

Eventually, I found a protocol that I know works really well. If I ever get a flare-up, I turn to the following recipe. I would like to hope it will help you too.
- ✓ Lactobillius Acidophilus
- ✓ Aloe Vera juice
- ✓ Silicol Gel

I recommend mixing my Aloe Vera Juice with the Silicol Gel in juice/milk/smoothie and taking the Lactobilius Acidophilus capsules with it. Within weeks you will find your IBS has calmed down.

A wonderful oil to help with stomach cramps and back cramps which often accompany IBS is a blend of Peppermint, Lavender, Frankincense and Clary Sage. Blend 10 drops Clary Sage, 5 of Lavender, 5 of Frankincense and 5 of Peppermint into 50mls of Grapeseed Oil. You can rub this blend onto your stomach, back and you can also bathe in 2 teaspoonfuls of the blend also to ease symptoms.

Tapping your Anxiety Away

Another therapy I found helped me on the spot so much so that I trained to become a Qualified Practitioner of it, is EFT.

This therapy works by tapping on Acupuncture points and works with the left and right sides of the brain too. You can use it anywhere as all it requires are the tips of your fingers for tapping your body with.

Firstly, rate the severity of your anxiety from 0-10 (10 being the worst)
- ✓ You then start tapping on the outside of your hand, saying an anchor sentence like: "Even though I'm feeling anxious, it's ok"
- ✓ Repeat 3 times whilst tapping on the outside of your hand.
- ✓ Then you tap the top of your head saying the word, "Anxious"
- ✓ Now tap in-between the eyebrows saying the word, "Anxious"
- ✓ Tap the outside of the eyebrow saying the word "Anxious"
- ✓ Then you tap under the eye and change to saying, "Letting it go"
- ✓ Now tap the cupids bow above the lip saying, "Letting it go"
- ✓ Tap in the middle fleshy part of your chin under your lip saying, "Letting it go"
- ✓ Then you tap the fleshy part of your collar bone saying, "Letting it go"
- ✓ Now you tap under your armpit saying, "Letting it go"
- ✓ Then you tap each of your fingers from pinky to thumb each time saying, "Letting it go".

You then tap on top of your hand under your pinky. Keep tapping here whilst you close your eyes, take a deep breath in and out, hum a tune, count to 5, open your eyes, roll your eyes around to the left then roll your eyes around to the right, breathe in deeply and out deeply. Stop.

Now rate your anxiety. You should find it has gone down. You can do this with anything, it helps to be as specific as possible. So, if the anxiety is making you feel panicky then change the work "anxious" to "panicky" or "worried" or "tearful". Whatever emotion you are feeling, say that as the anchor statement.

I still use this method today when I am about to teach and am feeling a little nervous and it never fails to help me. I urge you to seriously try it even though you may feel very silly doing it. Again, if you feel you would benefit from having a personal session with me guiding you through it to ensure you use the right statements etc then please do contact me to arrange this.

Breathing Your Anxiety Away

I stumbled across a breathing method which for many people has greatly helped their anxiety, called the Butyeko Breathing Method.

I'd heard about Butyeko breathing minimising the effects of asthma too, but I personally found it really confusing pinching my nose, nodding my head, holding my breath etc etc, so I created a simpler breathing technique and it worked! You alternate nose then mouth breathing to a count of 4.

1. Close your mouth & breath in slowly through your **nose** to a count of 4
2. Hold for a count of 4
3. Breath out **slowly** through your **nose** to a count of 4
4. Breath in again through your **nose** to a count of 4
5. Breath out **slowly** through your **mouth** to a count of 4
6. Breath in through your **mouth** for a count of 4 then hold,
7. and start the whole cycle again.
8. Keep doing this cycle until you start feeling calmer.

Whilst running my Apothecary shop and also offering a mail order service for my products (as word got around about the success of them helping people), I was also asked to work with children with special needs using my techniques. I loved this so much that I decided to train with a formal teaching qualification.

This led me down the route of initially working with primary school children, following which, I spent the next 15 years teaching Complementary Therapies in Clinical Practice to Health and Social Care students at a College in Cambridge, UK whilst also teaching at The Deakin Teaching and Learning Centre, Cambridge University Hopsital, UK.

I adored working with the students, inspiring them to achieve their dreams, until one evening I awoke in the middle of the night having heard my Mum's voice in a dream say the words, "Rachel, I'm dying".

I had not had a premonition in years, so I thought it was maybe just a dream worrying, because my Mum had come back into our lives 3 months after I had given birth to our twins, and they were now 3 years old.

Maybe I was worried about losing her again as my Husband and my Mum had rekindled their friendship, and my girls truly adored their Grandma Susan, and I absolutely loved my Mum spending weekends with us and also being at the other end of the phone often several times a day!

Sadly, my premonition came true, and my Mum discovered she had Endometrial Stromal Sarcom; 5 weeks after she was told it was terminal, she passed.

So once again, I experienced grief and loss but this time it was permanent.

Try to see the positive in everything

I had always been encouraged to try and see the positive in everything.

Two weeks after my Mum's death, we moved to a cottage in the middle of a beautiful wood. I spent a year juggling my job whilst also grieving and so I decided to work on myself; I was enveloped in the darkness of losing my Mum and I needed to do something about it.

Eventually, I left my teaching job, after 15 years it was time for a change, and for the following 6 months I threw myself into organising a large charity event in my Mums memory. I called it The Lifestyle and Wellbeing Show, and I wanted to raise awareness for Sarcoma and also to help promote over 100 small wellbeing businesses – as I believe Prevention is better than Cure.

My Mum had always taught me to be a strong woman and always try to find something positive even from the most negative of situations, so this is what I did. I was surprised to receive national coverage and was even awarded a Mumpreneur award – my Mum would have been proud.

Grieving in the woods & Getting Help with my Health Anxiety

I don't believe the fact we ended up moving to the woods was any accident, as I found myself using nature, the trees and walking as a remedy to my grieving. I cried uncontrollably for days and days; this went on for months.

I visited my GP, who was wonderful. I will forever be grateful to this wonderful doctor called Dr Siriwadena, who transferred an hour's worth of patients to another GP to sit and listen to me pour my heart out.

I was temporarily prescribed anti-depressants as I realised I could not fully function without some short-term help. Then my anxiety returned big time. This time it was different, rather than showing itself in breathless anxiety attacks and asthma, it came as health anxiety. I started constantly worrying about something happening to my Husband, or one, or both of my twins. If my Husband said he had indigestion, I would go into a panic. 'What if he was having a heart attack?'

One time, one of my twins had a really foul-smelling nostril (it turned out she had shoved a small craft pom-pom up her nose and it had got stuck and had to be removed at the hospital), but I convinced myself she had something serious. Another time, my other twin had some flea bites from a farm cat in the woods that she and her sister had befriended, the bites were itching and scarring so I convinced myself she could have a blood disorder and that was why the itching was not healing.

My health anxiety was getting out of control and affecting everyday life. The minute I felt worried about something, I would get a physical reaction like a freezing sensation which would shoot up to my head, then I would get palpitations and go into panic mode. So, I self-referred for CBT sessions.

Anyone can do this, you call up your GP and ask for the telephone number to self-refer for CBT. CBT (Cognitive Behavioural Therapy) is highly effective at helping you add rationale and logic to your illogical anxieties by using specific tools.

One of the best tools I would like to share with you is The Health Anxiety Thought Record. The template is below, it basically allows you to record your anxious thought and rate its severity and then look at a more rational explanation for the situation. I use this even today both on myself as well as my clients, I believe once you realise you have anxiety, you will sadly always have that tendency but if you have the tools and techniques to help, it will make your life more manageable. Try it for yourself.

Situation Date & Time	Trigger for Health Anxiety	Emotion rate 0-100%	Negative Thought State belief 0-100%	How I responded	Rational response to negative thought	Outcome Re-Rate belief of Negative thought 0-100%

As I have experienced intense anxiety in the past, again caused through loss, I am able to return to my roots and create my own treatment plan incorporating all the things I have trained in over the last 20 years: Tapping, Aromatherapy, Crystals, CBT, and Reflexology.

My girls and I take baskets, walk through the woods and collect what is needed. I have taught them about oils, so we make blends. Although still young, my girls miss my Mum and could initially also sense my intense emotions when she first passed, so burning the oils, tapping and with me doing the CBT work, helped us all, including my Husband Clive, who has been my rock through my battles with anxiety and who now has three very emotional females in the house to calm at times too!

Our Mind holds the Key to everything

Over my years of teaching healthcare, my training and also my personal experiences, I have realised the key to everything is THE MIND.

The mind is the most powerful thing we possess, and it affects every single aspect of our lives. We need only think of the placebo effect to realise this (our mind tells us a pill is going to work because it believes it is the real thing, and it works).

A survey carried out by MIND UK discovered that 3 out of 4 GP visits are actually linked to stress and depression, even if your appointment was primarily due to a physical issue. So although using natural ways to heal physical issues is amazingly helpful, the most important and powerful way of permanently healing a situation is by going within, and this is probably the hardest thing to do which is why we all try to look externally for solutions and quick fixes.

My time in the woods made me realise that by going within, asking my body and listening to the responses would I only then, truly heal.

During painful times in life, whether it be emotional pain or physical pain, you need to truly go into your feelings. Here are some ways of doing this.

Ask your body and you will get the answers

Sit quietly, alone, with no distractions; you are going to need to give yourself at least half an hour to do this. So if it means even sitting in the car or going for a walk and sitting on a bench, do it.

Take a few deep breaths in to centre yourself.

If your pain is physical, place your hands on where the pain is right now and leave them there for a few moments, you can still do this with emotional pain too by asking your body where it feels the emotion. Then ask yourself when the pain or emotional feeling first began, what was happening at that time, then just sit back and wait for your answers to come. You will find that a memory will come. Just experience that memory and all the emotions that come with it. This is your first step to healing your physical pain.

One of my clients had experienced a bad fall and knocked her shoulder, she was experiencing pain in her shoulder and subsequently pain in her back, followed by daily headaches. These physical symptoms are what had brought her to see me, yet when we did this powerful exercise, she experienced the emotions around the fall; she had been rushing (as we all do), trying to do too many things at once. Trying to take a cheque to the bank before it closed whilst making a phone call and she tripped and fell. Putting her hand out jolted her shoulder.

The emotion she experienced initially was anger at herself for falling, but once we went deeper, the anger moved to sadness at being alone and having to juggle so much just to survive, this then moved to feelings of loss as she had just split up from a long-term relationship. Once we worked on each of these emotions, the pain got less and less. So, you can see how although the initial pain was physical it had so many other emotions connected to it.

The slightest jolt of our emotions can affect us for years later without us even realising but by going within, taking time to ask and listen to our bodies, we can get so much information on how to heal ourselves. I find in my work, I am the guide to helping you get to those hidden causes, but I want to recommend that you try this exercise as you will be amazed at what you get from it.

Suppressed emotions in our body can create muscular tension which leads to stress if it not resolved at the time. Our minds and our bodies are so connected that many people following years of research have actually found reoccurring links between parts of the body and specific emotions, for example:

✓ Pain in the thumbs can be linked to control issues
✓ Pain in the knees or hips has been linked to not feeling supported
✓ Issues with the kidneys has been linked to Fear
✓ Issues with the lungs has been linked to Grief & Loss, as was my case.

Our emotions get stored in our bodies and if we haven't been able to deal with the emotions at those times when the issues first began, then we push them down further and further, and then we find something else happens and we push that down on top and before we know it after years of pushing things down and 'getting on with life' something more major occurs which jolts us in to looking at things.

We need to literally peel each layer back, layer after layer after layer. It can be daunting but so, so worth it. You may find things which you thought were small at the time, actually had a lasting impact on you.

When I was at Primary school, I was carrying a few extra pounds and was made fun of because of this. I hated that time at PE when teams were chosen; I would always be the last one to be picked. When you think back, it is such a small thing, but when I started to look within at healing myself, I realised my ongoing panic at being judged by people as not being good enough had initially stemmed from those times. Once I dealt with it, my feelings concerning judgement became less and less. But can you see how something so small can actually have such a big impact? I now know I am beautiful no matter what size I am, and should my daughters ever experience this same issue I now know that tapping on the emotion at the time will stop it from becoming a deep-seated problem.

By going within, you can get all the answers. It is sometimes difficult to not feel so overwhelmed with the situation that you don't know where to begin, and you might find getting help from a therapist to guide you, is what you need, but please try the above exercise as a starting point and go from there.

You may find going within, that your body or your intuition tells you to take some form of action. I had this after years of experiencing a strange spasm in one of my toes, it would just randomly go into a spasm and cross over the other toe next to it. I had just put it down to the shoes I had been wearing. Then I started becoming quite forgetful; again I just put it down to juggling lots of things as we all do, especially with children. Then one day, I did the above exercise and my intuition told me to go get a blood test. So I did. It was discovered that I was excessively deficient in B12.

B12 defficiency is a really common thing especially in women. The side effects can be spasming, numbness or tingling extremities, forgetfulness, anxiety, IBS type symptoms, light-headedness, tiredness, depression, palpitations, cracks at the sides of the mouth the list goes on.

I had been experiencing most of these symptoms but as I said, I just put it down to life pressures. It was only when I went within and asked my body that I discovered my B12 deficiency was a possible cause for many of my health-related issues. Believe it or not, you can even do this with animals by placing your hands on them and asking for an energy connection to what is going on. Try not to push your logical answers or listen to your ego telling you this is silly.

Just trust the messages you receive. Our bodies are amazing and we should trust them more.

So, over the years, I have continued to teach, treat wonderful clients, including animals as well as people. I deliver workshops, offer help online and create beautiful products to help with both emotional issues as well as physical issues using oils, crystals and herbs, (My Mum and Grandma would be proud!) alongside products to specifically help reduce anxiety for children as well as adults.

I create Worry Jars, Little Pots of Positivity and Workbooks and I now spend my time doing fairs with the products my now 8-year old twins, Eleanor and Isabel, helped make with our aptly named Ella & Issy Botanicals range.

I also create personal remedies and deliver workshops both online and in person, as well as offering Anxiety coaching for both personal & group sessions for children as well as adults. If you would like my help with either an Emotional issue or a Physical issue, please contact me.

Our Path is Our Purpose and I wish to help you with yours too. I hope by sharing a little of my story, it will help give you some comfort as well as some tools and techniques to help you on your path also.

Thank you for reading.
Love & Hugs.
Rachel Pernak-Brennon

www.eibotanicals.co.uk for all our beautiful Ella & Issy Botanicals products, workbooks & worry jars for children. You can also find out about how to book personal sessions, workshops and online mentoring from this link too, as well as having personal blends created to help you.

The caterpillar thought her life was ending

Then her wings grew

And she flew.

HEALING THE PAST
TO CONCEIVE A MIRACLE
By
Becky Jones

I have suffered with my periods right from the start, at age 13 to be precise; that very first bleed brought with it so much pain and sickness and fear. I had been well versed in what to expect in relation to bleeding from my special feminine place and the biology behind it, however there was no warning for the horrors that would accompany it.

One of my strongest memories from my teens is my younger brother walking in to find me on all fours on the kitchen floor, puffing and panting and screaming in agony, grey as a sheet and sweating. My Brother ran to get my Mum and I recall him shouting as he ran, "Mum, I think Becky is having a baby in the kitchen!" I was 14 and definitely not pregnant. I was merely on my period.

By age 15, Mum took me to the GP and they put me on the oral contraceptive. The Doctor said I must have a low pain threshold and was a bit of a hypochondriac because all women have pain with their periods!! I recall thinking how I was the only girl that had to take time off school during my monthlies and the only one to feel sick and nearly pass out. I knew intuitively something wasn't right but couldn't get anyone to listen.

The pill seemed to control things until I reached my 20's and at this point despite being on the pill my periods became painful again. Doctors changed my meds several times but to no avail. I kept getting told there was nothing wrong with me, I just had to grin and bear it, after all periods hurt!!!

Eventually my mum offered to come with me to the GP and insisted on a referral to see a Gynecologist.

After what seemed like the longest wait, I got an appointment at the gynae clinic and following the examination was delivered with the devastating news that I had a condition called Endometriosis, which might affect me having children. I was 24yrs old, had just bought my first home and was about to get married and start a family.

All I ever wanted to be in life was a loving devoted Mummy and Wife. I felt like my world just fell apart.

Over the next few years I underwent 3 operations. Surgeons discovered that my right ovary and fallopian tube were completely adhered to the back wall and my right tube was blocked and damaged. They said my insides looked like at some point I had endured a massive internal bleed that had left congealed blood sticking things together. I was sent away with instructions to try and get pregnant soon because time was against me and if I needed fertility treatment I would need to go on the long waiting list!

My chances felt pretty miserable hearing that news and I left feeling broken. At the time I was working as a Business Development Executive for a multi-national insurance company and the stress was exacerbating my condition. I had so much time off work due to Endo, I ended up losing my job and sunk deep into depression.

The years went by and I had several miscarriages and several failed attempts at fertility treatment. I felt broken. I was meant to be a Mummy, I just had to fix this.

I started listening to my higher self and meditating and decided to go to a spiritual healer. As soon as he started work on me he described seeing the blood congealed in my abdomen and described how my ovary and tube were stuck. He said spirit was telling him that it related to accidents and trauma as a child. I was gobsmacked.

I remembered when I was about 7 years old I fell off my horse whilst riding up the mountains. I landed on my privates on a rocky area and bled for days.

My mum assumed I was starting my period early so at that point I wasn't taken to see a Doctor.

About a year later I had another fall whilst horse-riding and landed on my tailbone. I could barely walk home. Suddenly the mess inside started to make sense. But.... how to fix it?

At this point in my life I was really exploring my Psychic/Healing gifts and I started to meditate and tap into my past lives. One of the lives I was shown was of me as a woman in a very poor farm life in USA where I had died traumatically, giving birth all alone.

Suddenly all the miscarriages and failed fertility treatment made sense. My soul was scared to allow me to carry a pregnancy to term because it feared me dying during childbirth, like in the previous life.

I set to work researching and self-healing. In the meantime, I was booked in for another operation to have my right fallopian tube removed and more endometriosis burnt off my right ovary. When I woke up from the operation I cried so hard. 7 years of trying for a baby was failing with 2 fallopian tubes and now my chances had been halved!

After a few days of tears, I decided to snap out of it and I gave my body an ultimatum. I connected with my womb and told her that I did not have to fear the past repeating itself; we were safe to conceive and deliver a beautiful baby and what's more we deserved that blessing. I told my body if I didn't get pregnant by the end of the year I was going to stop trying to conceive and would take medication to stop the fertility treatment, as I had enough of suffering every month.

I meditated as I healed from the operation and sat with my Moon Stone crystal on my womb area with my hand over it and visualised myself healing and empowering my womb.

Just 4 weeks after I had my right fallopian tube taken out, I missed my period. I had only tried to conceive once since the operation but here I was waking up at 4am feeling very strange and sitting in the bathroom looking at a positive pregnancy test. I was elated and scared because I had been here several times so far and I just prayed the healing had worked.

The night that I had conceived I sat with my Moon Stone with my hand over my womb area and I visualised myself conceiving and lived the excitement I would feel in that moment.

A couple of weeks after conception I had a vision that engaging in sex would force miscarriage and as soon as my (then) Husband started making demands for physical attention I mysteriously started to bleed. Doctors had no idea why I was bleeding, but scans showed my baby was fine.

I rang my Mum to tell her that I felt having sex would cause a miscarriage and my Mum confessed she had a feeling that I was right. So this time around I vowed not to have any sex during this pregnancy. My relationship with my Husband was already facing difficulties due to his lack of compassion and I made it quite clear I was not prepared to jeopardize this pregnancy, so I was sorry but there would be no sex. He reluctantly agreed.

My pregnancy progressed without any major complications and for the first time in my life I felt as though I had found my purpose in life.

A week over my due date my waters broke during my sleep on a Thursday night. My contractions started on the following night, but my baby girl didn't make her entrance into the world until the Sunday afternoon!!

I felt as though my body/soul was still terrified to go through labour, but we got there in the end and I safely delivered my gorgeous healthy baby girl.

To safeguard us both, my baby and I had to stay in hospital for 3 days due to me developing an infection and losing half my blood during delivery. It really did feel like history was trying very hard to repeat itself!!

After 7 years of struggling, I finally held my precious baby girl in my arms. I can't begin to describe how blessed I felt and still do to this day. I know how lucky I am to have been given the gift of Motherhood. Every night I thank my Daughter for choosing me to be her Mummy in this life. She in turn thanks me for choosing to be her Mummy. I strongly believe if I hadn't done the regression and healing work I might never have been blessed with my beautiful baby girl. ♥

Shortly after having my Daughter, I trained and qualified in Reflexology and various other holistic therapies and healing techniques. It's a dream of mine to be able to help other women heal and achieve their goal of becoming a Mummy.

-End-

"Always remember that age is just a number and it's never too late to start over and follow your soul's desire."

Cath B

ADOPTION AND ABANDONMENT
By
Linda Chester

Can you feel it?
That tiny spark that's growing, drawing me closer and closer to you. Being with you makes me feel safe and pure.

Can you feel it?
This special month where love grows and flows into something wonderous and beautiful, creating a delight in my soul and a fire in yours that spreads across the sky like sunset on a summer's evening. Such passion, such depth and fulfilment.

Can you sense it?
Like blossom and leaves on budding trees, with a promise of life and dreams and desires. Emotion runs high on the tide of innocence perceived to be taken, and not given willingly of love and desire, a need for passion in this pure soul.

Can you sense it?
The blame, the shame, the hiding away for fear of others' destructive onslaught of verbal cruelty, and so the heat and pressure continues like a pounding of the waves on a stormy night.

Can you sense it?
You have felt it, like the leaves that fade and fall, so do you; falling under the relentless gales that blow and howl, only to send you away.

You have gone, my soul cries, for now I am forced into the bright light, not knowing, not feeling, not understanding. Reluctantly I enter this new world, I am unsure, I touch this new world with my toes. As I emerge from the darkness, my body follows.....I am born.

I can't feel it, I can't sense it; that link of love we shared for 9 months.

That link that kept me safe and nourished, that link that talked to me as if she knew me…. I can't feel it any more. Such an abrupt severing; will I ever feel such love again?

I am abandoned, an unloved soul that's floundering in a strange environment.

Who will love me?
Who will help me become who I am meant to be?

All around me are strange, unfamiliar sounds. Voices of caring but not of loving, I am nourished and warm, but otherwise there is nothing that compares with the love I felt from within the womb… and so this continues.

I am taken from one strange place to another; we are in the beautiful countryside. It is cold. I see two people. Can I feel it? Can I feel a spark from one of these people? Yes I can. Oh joy, I am feeling again and I am drawn to the man. There is a definite spark. I feel kindness but also another intangible feeling from the woman. It is not unkind but neither is it a spark, it is more of perhaps a duty, an obligation maybe. I don't know. Perhaps it will become clearer over time, perhaps it won't.

I have been placed in the care of these people who perhaps, have to find their way and do their best to nourish both my body and soul, with only the guidance from others to help them, their perceived soul development yet no ability to follow their own soul connection and calling. They must conform to what is expected of them and do it. It is a learning process for all of us.

Why am I so different from other souls who are of the same age as me? Why do they not feel or search for the spark as I am doing?

What is my function in this environment? I feel so deeply, yet I am told to grow up and not be so sensitive. Grow up?! Does this mean that when I get taller I will understand and be more like them? Does this mean that I will not feel things as I do now?

It's very painful to try and understand why I should try not to feel, but maybe I should try this; maybe then I will be like everybody else and the spark will ignite and glow.

I try and conform; I learn the piano. It is not quite up to the standard of others; I try my best within the educational system, who are doing what is expected of them. There is no individuality or encouragement to develop what I can do easily, only 'can do better'.

Although reading came very easily to me, I enjoy singing and music. I am told I can't sing because my voice is too weak. So I stopped singing.

I go to chapel every Sunday. This is so alien to me although I cannot understand why it feels as it does. I am fearful and discouraged, but remain respectful and do what is 'expected'.

I fear I am dying inside because no-one is recognising the spark except for the male. We communicate very little verbally, but there is that spark so at least I feel I have something. We have a non-verbal closeness.

I watch the female talking to other souls and to animals and wonder why she does not love me like that; maybe I am unlovable, maybe I am unworthy of anyone's love and attention. After all, I was abandoned, wasn't I?

I am never good enough at whatever I do, so perhaps I should stop trying.

I reach the conclusion that the Female is the ruling planet and both the Male and I are mere satellites circling continuously; I quietly withdraw into my own thoughts. Maybe, just maybe, I can find someone who will feed what my soul desires. Someone who does think that I am worthy and good enough; worthy of being listened to; worthy of being cherished.

Can you feel it?
That tiny spark that's growing, drawing me closer and closer to you.
Being with you makes me feel safe and pure.

Can you feel it?
Love grows and flows into something wonderous and beautiful, creating a delight in my soul and a fire in yours that spreads across the sky like sunset on a summer's evening. Such passion, such depth and fulfilment.

Can you sense it?
Like blossom and leaves on budding trees, with a promise of life and dreams and desires.

I found that person; oh such bliss, such a feeling of effervescence, I am full of joy. At last my whole existence is changing, I can be who I really want to be with this beautiful dark eyed, dark haired soul.

Sadly, the ruling planet told me that I must study and make something of my life, otherwise I will 'turn out' just like my Mother! I didn't understand this. What was wrong in loving and being loved? Of course, I wasn't conforming to what was 'the done thing' and fulfilling her expectations.

It seemed that I was maybe re-living my Mother's mistake. I think my soul satellite understood though, in fact, I know he did.

I didn't see my soul-mate for some time, I was devastated, crumbling, lost and fading. Once again abandoned; what could I possibly do to find completeness?

I wasn't good enough at anything, maybe I shouldn't even try? What was the alternative? OK, so I was unlovable; I wasn't good enough at anything. Maybe I shouldn't even try?!

Around this time, I became quite poorly and needed surgery; I spent a few weeks in hospital.

I realised that although I felt unloved, I was shown such compassion and care that I thought maybe I should try focusing on giving, and not expect to be loved for myself and my soul.

So, from this point on, I began a career in Nursing (which spanned over 40 years). There was fulfilment in giving and caring, but there was still something missing which my soul craved for. However, I actually felt soul-less at the same time.

I had moved away from home and the ruling planet's influence, but still there was the expectation of performing well. When I wasn't working, I was expected to come home whilst my friends were having fun. Oh my, will this ever, ever end? What was the way out? What can I do? If only I could find it, but I didn't even know at that time what it was that I was looking for.

I got married; there wasn't a hint of a spark, not even a glow but at that time it was a way out, and after all, I wasn't worthy or loveable, was I?!

So, life continued; working, giving, caring...apart from my work, there was absolutely nothing else. No new souls to bring into the world that I could love and cherish, who in turn would love me for who and what I am. It was a dim light in a very dark tunnel.

I became ill again, needed surgery and was dealt what I thought was the hardest blow of my life: I needed a hysterectomy! I would never have a connection with a young soul; never develop that soul connection further and watch it grow from a spark to a flame. The very essence of femininity was being taken away and dumped in the bin. My femininity had abandoned me! I was told that I would get over it and that I could adopt.

I wasn't even good enough to be a Mother!

Once I recovered, I returned to work and carried on with my career. I was working the night shift - and so was my Husband: with another female! I was unlovable and abandoned yet again! The story of my life really!

This time though, I was the one who did the abandoning; I left, although my soul was craving for something. I still didn't know what, but I was damned if I was going to sink. The ruling planet and religious elders were appalled with my behaviour. It just wasn't the thing to do, but I did it anyway.

Can you feel it?
That tiny spark that's growing, drawing me closer and closer to you; being with you makes me feel safe and pure.

Can you feel it?
Love grows and flows into something wonderous and beautiful, creating a delight in my soul and a fire in yours that spreads across the sky like sunset on a summer's evening; such passion, such depth and fulfilment.

Can you sense it?
Like blossom and leaves on budding trees, with a promise of life and dreams and desires.

I am loveable, my soul is awakened from the hidden depths of despair, my soulmate returned into my life...such euphoria!

I couldn't quite believe this, so I thought I may as well enjoy the bliss for as long as it lasted, and as long as I was loveable.

Being used to abandonment, I felt it would likely happen again!

Yet...

I willingly gave my heart and soul to this beautiful person and his 2 little boys. I still do, 33 years later.

He may not be as dark haired now as when we first met, but his soul shines through his eyes and we are in each other's hearts.

By reflecting and really trying to put myself in both my birth and adoptive mothers' situations, I had almost come to understand how things were or may have been at that time and appreciate that things were done for what seemed the best.

However, my soul was still seeking the elusive something. I became very interested in healing and complementary therapy, studied and qualified in a fair few therapies and healing modalities. Little did I know that this would be the start of another journey of discovery with pain, heartache, self-analysis and really, really compounded the belief that I was not worthy!

Who on earth did I think I was, that I believed my soul could actually connect to the greater source? That I had information that was held deep within my soul and other places? I slowly started to acknowledge that yes, perhaps I could, and am working on this every single day.

During the past 6 months, another beautiful soul has climbed aboard my soul train; I have been blessed to meet and work with Sam Lyndley and truly believe that she is the bridge to what I have been missing for all these years.

Through the 'Discover Your Purpose' group that Sam has created and leads, alongside regular mentoring with her, I am finally starting to acknowledge who I really am, what my soul is craving for and my soul purpose.

I have learnt with Sam, that despite not having a womb, the cellular energy is still there and that this is indeed the seat of intuition. Sam has introduced and shared her knowledge and efficacy of connecting with the womb, and how much she can teach us.

When I connected with this energy, I had such pain which I worked through; I have written my story from the womb space which is such an incredible place to be working from and as I write, the pain is almost gone.

My Soul is sparkling.

Another blessing is being given the opportunity by Andrea to contribute to this book; such heartfelt gratitude and thanks because putting all this down on paper has helped my healing process immensely.

Closing thoughts.
At no time during my childhood, development, call it whatever you wish, was I harmed in any physical or psychological way. This was simply part of my journey towards being able to reach out to others if they so wished. I had to go through this, so I will always hold love in my heart for both mothers.

My advice to you is to be strong, ask for help and listen to your intuition; you are worthy and loved.

Additional Information
Through my continuing healing, learning and development, there is so much that has and continues to play a big part on this journey. From music to poetry and inspirational quotes, I have listed some of my favourites below in no particular order. May it help you in the same way it helped me.

Native American drumming and flute music
Deva Premal & Gayatri Mantra - YouTube
Let it Be - The Beatles
Love My Life – Robbie Williams

> "When the power of love overcomes the love of power,
> the world will know peace."
> *Jimi Hendrix*

© Evelyn Whitebear, 2017

DESIDERATA
By
Max Ehrmann
© 1952

Go placidly amid the noise and haste,
and remember what peace there may be in silence.
As far as possible without surrender
be on good terms with all persons.
Speak your truth quietly and clearly;
and listen to others,
even the dull and the ignorant;
they too have their story.

Avoid loud and aggressive persons,
they are vexations to the spirit.
If you compare yourself with others,
you may become vain and bitter;
for always there will be greater and lesser persons than yourself.
Enjoy your achievements as well as your plans.

Keep interested in your own career, however humble;
it is a real possession in the changing fortunes of time.
Exercise caution in your business affairs;
for the world is full of trickery.
But let this not blind you to what virtue there is;
many persons strive for high ideals;
and everywhere life is full of heroism.

Be yourself.
Especially, do not feign affection.
Neither be cynical about love;
for in the face of all aridity and disenchantment
it is as perennial as the grass.

Take kindly the counsel of the years,
gracefully surrendering the things of youth.
Nurture strength of spirit to shield you in sudden misfortune.
But do not distress yourself with dark imaginings.

Many fears are born of fatigue and loneliness.
Beyond a wholesome discipline,
be gentle with yourself.

You are a child of the universe,
no less than the trees and the stars;
you have a right to be here.
And whether or not it is clear to you,
no doubt the universe is unfolding as it should.

Therefore be at peace with God,
whatever you conceive Him to be,
and whatever your labours and aspirations,
in the noisy confusion of life keep peace with your soul.

With all its sham, drudgery, and broken dreams,
it is still a beautiful world.
Be cheerful.
Strive to be happy.

CONVERSATION WITH MY GODDESS ENERGY (GE)
By
Linda Chester

GE: How wonderful to see that, at last, you have realized that although I am not here organically, my energy still remains. You were entering the goddess phase when we last spoke!!

ME: Thank you, I am really uncertain if this can be real because you are not there and haven't been for many years.

GE: Why have you taken so long to connect, you have had teachers, read many books and have medical knowledge?
I would guess that you have been angry with me for so long and have not even thought that my energy is still around.

ME: Yes, that is so true, I blamed you for me not being able to fulfil, what I saw as my purpose, and bring new life into the world. I blamed you for the pain you caused me every month, I blamed you when my flow was so painful that there were times I couldn't walk. I blamed you because I could and did bleed...every three weeks! The moon cycle was not something to be embraced at that time in my life, it was spoken of as being a nuisance, and just something that we had tolerate so tough luck if there were problems! I also blamed you for the loss of my feminine essence. I was glad when you were gone and I could get a life.... how wrong was I?!

GE: You talk of not being able to fulfil your purpose, I once held a soul spark for you, but the time and conditions were not conducive, so the spark returned to the soul group. You also talk about the loss of your femininity... I was there all along wasn't I, you just didn't want to recognise this because of your anger and blame.

ME: Yes, I understand that now, it is one of the many lessons I have learned and am still learning.

When I first connected with you, I had some pain and indeed, the whole energy around you felt as cold as ice; empty and dark. I almost didn't continue with the connection, but, you wouldn't let me ignore you would you?! I continued connecting, talking and using crystals.

GE: Once we made the connection, there was no way that I wanted to lose this so that's why I kept reminding you...I too can be persistent. So how are you feeling now that we have connected?

ME: I almost cannot believe how different I feel; softer, more tolerant, feminine and through talking to you, I have even more clarity of purpose.

GE: Please continue working with me, you are now entering the wise woman stage of your life, lots to learn still, but even more to give.

ME: Thank you, I will. I also ask your forgiveness for ignoring you for so long.

So, I have been working with the womb energy now for a couple of months. This has brought about profound change, increased clarity and heightened intuition. In fact all my senses are heightened and I am far more sensitive. I had one of the most profound experiences ever during the early hours of this morning whilst at work.

I was talking to a young lady via telephone, she was 6 weeks pregnant and seeking advice. During our conversation, I could feel my womb energy becoming really noticeable, just as if someone was blowing up a balloon. I could feel the shape, the colour and the energy, it was so warm. I competed my consultation and went outside for some fresh air.

I then became aware of a sort of 'bubbling' sensation and in a split second, believe that I had actually made contact with the energy of the soul seed which had returned to the soul group many, many years ago. I felt a feeling of completeness and have not fully processed this yet, but oh boy...such a loving energy.

-End-

NOBODY LISTENS TO ME
By
Linda Chester

I was a young student nurse, living 25 miles away from home for the first time. I was enjoying my training mostly but there were a couple of things that were making me feel quite miserable; I had a constant pain in my left side and the love of my life had married someone else.

I had seen various local doctors on a couple of occasions regarding this pain, only to be told that it was pre-menstrual, post-menstrual, ovulation, constipation and so on, basically just get on with it.

This one particular evening, my friends had gone out, I didn't want to go as I felt quite miserable and in pain and generally so fed up with all this, going over memories of my happy times with my first love. I had taken pain relief without much effect; I couldn't sleep. I remembered that I had some sleeping tablets which all of us took to overcome the transition from and to day and night shift. I also had a small amount of whiskey which someone had left in my room. So I took some sleeping tablets and couple of gulps of whiskey thinking, "If only I could go to sleep, things will be better when I wake up".

There were no thoughts of ending my life, just a break from this pain and feeling low.

My friends came home and I told them what I'd done, by this time, I was quite sleepy. Surprise, surprise, they took me to A&E, and from there, I was admitted to the mental health unit where I stayed for a number of weeks. I was asked what had caused me to take an overdose. I spoke truthfully about my physical pain and expressed that I had no suicidal intent and just wanted some escape from the physical pain.

I was given medication and in all honesty, I can only remember feeling as if I was outside myself looking in, with a feeling of being protected in some way; the experience was surreal.

I also remember my Father bought me the most beautiful dressing gown. I don't remember my Mother coming to see me very often and we never, ever referred to this period in my life. Eventually, I was discharged and went to stay with the family of someone who I had recently met. I couldn't face going home to rebuild my strength, although I still saw my parents.

Over time, I went back to work, had some quite strange looks and there were some derogatory comments such as, "Oh, she's the nutter".

I still had this pain but because I had been suffering on a previous occasion with mental health problems and it was documented in my notes. no-one listened, and even a consultant told me it was all in my head.

Some months later, I had been given a diagnosis and surgery was the only appropriate outcome at that time. This was after I had been seen by another consultant who conducted the appropriate investigations. I had great satisfaction seeing the look on my original consultant's face on the morning of my surgery during his ward round when he was told that I was going down to theatre for a hysterectomy. Whiter shade of pale does not even begin to describe the look on his face. Although this was a double-edged sword; I was sad at the thought of surgery but glad that I knew all along that there was something not right.

And so we come to the present day. In a mentoring session, Sam Lyndley triggered this memory which led me to research the medication I was prescribed for my depression. It seems they should never have been taken together, creating a lasting effect of insomnia.

Nobody listened to me and what I was feeling and why I was feeling this way, no words of comfort were ever given that I can remember; no hugs, no reassurance that in some way, things would work out.

I spoke to a young lady on the last night shift I worked, it was 3am, she was in floods of tears, she couldn't cope, she had mental health issues, she was the main carer for her mother who also had mental health issues and she said in her own words, "Nobody is listening to me". We were both in tears.

So my talk with Sam and the events that followed, have been beautifully cleansing for me; I know that I have totally healed that particular hurt. I know that I am able to connect with my womb energy, to Source and feel very blessed that I am able to do this and, above all, I know that I can listen and see beyond what's actually being said to me without judgement or prejudice.

If I can be of help in anyway at all to anyone I am here and will listen.

By the way, I have been married to my first love for 33 years in December 2017.

-End-

"If ever in doubt; listen to your inner wisdom and let your soul guide you.
She knows."

Cath B

FOR MY DAUGHTER
By
Lynsey Doel

Let her sleep upon the mossy earth, for her to awaken and gaze upon the cosmos above.

The swirling balls of bright dust and gas and miracles abundant above her.

Let her feel the soil beneath her nails and the soft grass between her digits, feeling the soul of her very earth complete her.

Taste the rain with her tongue and feel the wind whip her hair into a frenzied wildness.

Let her soul be delighted and warmed by the rays on her skin.

Let her not forsake these pleasures.

Let her know and practice them.

This is my wish for her.

Let it be, my beautiful girl.

-End-

SACRED WOMEN
By
Lynsey Doel

Sacred Women, I call you to arms.

Bring with you your darkness and mystery. She is a part of you, as much as your blood is vital in your veins.

Find comfort, not fear in the shadows that she brings.

We are the cocoon, We are the Womb. We are a vessel of spirit and life. We are divinity.

Revel in your primal nature. Roar, Weep, Laugh, Make Love.

Re-member, Re-claim; your roots are calling you.

Feel no shame. Wrap the arms of your darkness around your very being and love it fiercely.

Let the moon illuminate and guide through the darkest of shadows.

Be still, Dance, Weave words.

Make magic and be your very innate, sacred, beautiful you.

-End-

REIKI AND ME
By
Jo Prince

It has been nearly twenty years since Reiki found me and it seems incredible the changes that have taken place within me.

I was so full of negative energies and depression from an abusive marriage and despair at not meeting a new partner. Reiki gave me hope and a way to heal the emotional damage.

Where to begin, when so much has happened? Well, surely from the beginning.

I left an abusive marriage with two young children, returned to college and qualified as a teacher, found a job, bought a lovely house, found fantastic friends and had the support of a loving family. From an outsider looking in I was very fortunate but I still felt empty and tied to my past and emotional baggage from my marriage.

I did not feel like I had achieved anything worthwhile and was still full of self-doubt and depression. I was still searching, (as now I can look back and see with open eyes) and although I had made many achievements I felt the negative energies from my past were stopping me from moving on and celebrating the new life I had made for myself and my two beautiful children.

Then I got my calling.

One Easter a leaflet on Reiki literally fell at my feet from a book I had not opened in a while, so I had already read it, but it had made no impression on me at the time.

That week a friend had been telling me about a lady who did Reiki and how marvellous it was, and I kept seeing adverts and signs outside shops, all advertising Reiki.

As I read the leaflet I said out loud, "OK, I get the message; I need Reiki!"

My first Reiki treatment was so relaxing and for the first time I felt that I could move on. I had not been able to see a light at the end of my tunnel and I did not know how to move forward. The Reiki highlighted all the baggage I was carrying and I made a conscious effort to let it go.

What a relief to find that there was a reason for all the self-doubt and negativity. I was so moved by my experiences that I immediately booked to do a Reiki 1 course, with the same practitioner. This was some way off, so I rang local colleges and put my name down on their waiting lists too.

Within a month a cancellation at a college gave me the opportunity to do the course. I felt that this was no coincidence. The feeling of relaxation and hope that followed cannot be described. The friends that I made that day are still practicing Reiki with me, in fact we returned to the same Reiki Master to do our 2nd Degree course.

Reiki has brought to light many personal issues and helped me release many tears. It has helped me put the past behind me and accept that everything I have had to deal with was for a reason.

From a Christian upbringing, I found it hard to justify my Reiki Healer title, with Christian friends disputing where the healing comes from.

But for me, I am living a life to help others, sharing God's love and bringing support and comfort wherever I can. Surely this is the life God would want us to live? The bible speaks of healing and I feel that we are doing just that.

I feel Reiki is more universally acceptable these days and people without a devout religious background are more likely to seek Reiki than perhaps go to a church for healing.

With Reiki I am able to help a wider range of people as so many people are feeling challenged; Reiki has in turn helped me to understand the necessity of all my own suffering, so I now have greater empathy when helping others.

I can even thank my ex-Husband for our dysfunctional relationship, as without hitting such a personal low I would never have applied to college, to prove to us both that I still have what it takes, or been so full of negativity to seek Reiki to alleviate it. I would not have my children either.

In fact, I can go so far as to thank him for the wonderful life that I have now. If you asked me to say anything like that a year ago, I would have laughed in disbelief! Time and Reiki does indeed heal.

Fast forward to the present, and I have met my life partner and found love; a comfortable safe love. I have two more beautiful children and at last I am living the life I had always hoped for.

I am a Reiki Master Teacher with regular clients and feel an inner peace that I radiate to others through my healing.

Who knows what other issues I may need to still deal with. Who knows where Reiki will take me next. I look forward to each day and feel extremely grateful that I was brought to Reiki. I accept that for today, this very minute, I am right where I am supposed to be.

So, my message for you today, is:

Just for today, do not worry.
Just for today, do not anger.
Just for today, treat all living things equally.
Just for today, earn an honest living.
Just for today, be grateful for all you have.

Just for today, this one day will turn into two when you do the same tomorrow, then three, four, fourteen, twenty-one and before you know it, your life will have changed – for the better. You'll see.

GUIDED MEDITATION FOR LETTING GO
By
Jo Prince

"Now, for those who want something a little deeper, what follows is a guided meditation. If you are unfamiliar with meditating, just follow the instructions and relax; you're in safe hands".

I use this meditation for people who are carrying a lot of past baggage and issues that they are struggling to let go of. It helps to release negativity.

You can read it out loud and record it, then play it back to yourself. Or have someone read it to you.

Firstly, find a quiet place where you will not be disturbed. Sit comfortably. Take three deep breathes and relax your shoulders. Picture all your worries leaving with those deep breathes out. Close your eyes.

Meditation
Picture yourself standing in a beautiful pasture of green grass and wild flowers. Look down at your feet and see the greenery touching your toes, feel the earth under your feet. The warmth of the sun relaxes you as you breathe in deeply smelling the wild flowers and fresh air.

In the distance you hear a buzz of a passing bee. Far above you, you hear the call of a bird, circling overhead. You feel calm and relaxed.

As you walk slowly through the beautiful pasture, you notice the gentle noise of bubbling water. You wander slowly towards the water and notice a clear gurgling stream with clear water disappearing off in to the distance. The sound of the water is mesmerising, and you feel even more relaxed.

It is such a beautiful day and you know it is time to let go of any baggage that has been weighing you down. You are safe. You are ready.

In the stream you notice a box bobbing about on the water. It is tied to the bank by a beautiful ribbon. You look at the box. What is it made of? What colour ribbon is attached? Take hold of the ribbon and feel the box gently tugging at your hand to be released down the stream.

Take a deep breath and fill yourself with love. When you are ready I want you to imagine putting your baggage in the box. It could be hurt from a partner. It could be anger or resentment. Anything that is negative and is weighing you down; only you know what needs to be 'Let Go'.

Now place it with love in the box. Many things may come up as you off-load, and that is fine. You have carried this around for long enough now. It serves no purpose. It is time to let it go.

When you are ready, take another deep breath and with love, gently release the ribbon and watch your box disappear off down the stream.

All your worries - all your negativity - all your past issues that you have been holding onto are leaving you.

Give thanks for all these things and feel grateful that you have released them.

You are feeling lighter and filled with love as you release the negativity that has been weighing you down. Take a deep breath and know that you have done the right thing and you are free to move on.

Walk slowly back to the meadow. The sun warms your shoulders and it feels so good. You notice beautiful butterflies dancing in the sky. You may feel like dancing with them or skipping as you feel light and loved.

You may like to lie down in the beautiful grass and flowers and enjoy the feeling of freedom. Know that you are loved and blessed.

When you are ready, take three deep breathes. Wiggle your toes. Wiggle your fingers. And slowly come back into the room.

Well done. Trust that you have released your negativities with love.

-End-

HOW TO SHIFT FORWARD INTO BEING YOUR TRUE SELF, RELEASING OLD PATTERNS OF BEING

Taking Care of Yourself from the Inside Out
- A Beginning –
By
Jayne Turner

My name is Jayne Turner, I am a Holistic Counsellor and Published Author.

I have many stories that I could share about my own journey in becoming spiritually awakened and connected with myself. Although my stories may resonate with you, my stories do not define me. It is the learning that I have taken from journeying within, which is the biggest gift I can give you.

My hope is that you will feel able to find your own steps to be your true self using the steps I have taken to help guide you.

≈

The most vital and important lesson I have learned through my own personal development and training in becoming a counsellor is, self-care. This is not an easy thing to learn due to conditioning, self-worth and life experiences.

It began for me when I realised as a sensitive and empath, I was always there for others even when I was empty. My vessel never had a chance to replenish. Always a giver but not to myself. Through my own journey I have realised there were four main elements which were really holding me back from being my true self.

1) Negative self-talk
2) Lack of value for my own self care
3) My relationship with myself
4) Trusting my intuition and trusting the process

The first step was to become aware of the inner conversations with myself. I noticed how negative I really was, how I berated myself, not allowing myself the compassion and understanding I so easily gave to others.

This was not something that happened overnight, it was gentle mindfulness, really listening to how I spoke to myself and catching the thoughts as they came. When I started catching those negative thoughts I could become present with them. I began to realise I could change them to something more compassionate, more loving of myself. I could change how I related to myself by becoming more accepting and understanding.

Step 1

For example, I'd say, "Well you didn't make a very good job of that, you really are not good enough". Catching that thought, noticing how it felt in my body and then talking to myself as if I was a friend I'd reply with, "That was difficult to do, but you tried. Well done for trying, what have you learned? How could you do this differently next time?" This felt very different to receive.

I could begin to give myself permission to be imperfect. Through continuously practising this, I have now got to a point where most of the time my inner critic/negative voice is far gentler, forgiving and accepting. There are times when I take a few steps backward though. Any muscle can show signs of weakness; old wounds can re-materialise. When this happens, I notice myself feeling disconnected, with low energy and even depressed. When I become aware of this I stop and pause. I ask myself, "How have you been speaking to yourself?" and straight away I hear "negatively". So, I gently remind myself I have a choice. No one else is my voice, I can be 'my best friend or my worst enemy'.

Step 2

The next step was looking at how I value and care for myself, which became evident to me through my exploration of my self-talk/inner critic. I realised I had not been allowing myself what 'I' need.

This has many levels to it, from personal and professional boundaries. Really listening to my body and recognising how I hadn't connected with my physicality.

I hadn't been nourishing myself through making poor food choices, and not giving my body regular exercise. (This was personal; I had to really allow myself to discover what I enjoyed and could financially support. Yet it has enabled me to stay motivated and continue with my investment in my body).

Through my own experiential exploration, I began to put in place my own 'circle of care' so I can support myself emotionally, physically and spiritually.

This has been intrinsic in my wellbeing and continues to grow and change and develop. I feel like I can really hold a space for myself. I can say no to others needs. I recognise I can't support anyone if I am not giving myself what I need.

Step 3

I was beginning to build a deeper connection with myself.

I had started to learn about who I really was not 'who I should be'.

Often, we search outside of ourselves, seeking clarity from others and validation.

What I now know is it's all there within me, but this is so hard to find when we become disconnected with ourselves.

When we can fully connect and be present with ourselves moment by moment, we can become gently curious with our triggers and emotions. We can find the answers we seek.

Sometimes it is our connection with others which enables us to see what we can't otherwise see and through experiencing that, we can then connect with our own truth.

The most important relationship we will ever have is with ourselves. We are the only ones who will be forever in our lives from the first and last breath we take.

Step 4

After deepening my connection with myself I could recognise my intuition; what just felt right or wrong and what or who I was drawn to or felt a tension from (sometimes like a physical force).

When we begin to have a deeper connection with ourselves we start having a deeper connection with everything around us.

Have you ever experienced coincidence, serendipity, those amazing light bulb moments when everything just feels exactly as its meant to be? Yet it comes and goes and can be so hard to maintain.

The more I began to trust my intuition the more these moments occurred. I had to take the biggest leap of faith in my life.

Everything in my personal/spiritual development had led me to this point. I had a choice. I could play it safe, and continue to feel something was missing in my life, unfulfilled. Or I could take this opportunity with both my eyes and heart wide open.

To change something, we need to be courageous and make those changes.

I learnt to be grateful for all that I have, not resentful for what I don't.

I became grateful for all the experiences I had received, good and bad. They were what led me to my life-changing moment.

I believe making mistakes are not a sign of failure. For me failing is being unwilling to try.

When I make mistakes, I am now willing to learn deeply from them (sometimes I must make the same mistake several times to recognise the lesson. Sometimes it may feel I am relearning the same mistake. Yet at deeper reflection I realise it's another layer to the lesson from a different perspective).

So here I am walking forward sometimes stumbling, sometimes running, sometimes crawling but I am moving forward. Sometimes I must pause, this journey of self is not an easy one.

There are many times I have wanted to step off! I know I can't. It is through this journey I have been able to really recognise my purpose.

I am and have always been a counsellor. Only now can I really be of service because I have experienced the journey I invite my clients to travel.

I am by no means fixed, we are all a work in progress. I believe my journey has been about how I can walk forward. How I became my best friend and my true self.

Trust is the most empowering concept to carry us forward. 'Trust the process' and all will be revealed, exactly at the right time and just when we need it to be. We don't always get what we want but we always get what we need (to learn about ourselves).

Overleaf is a short poem which I think helps to encapsulate all that I have written. My biggest hope is that some if not all my experience will resonate with you, enabling you to feel you are not alone and that you too can walk on your own path to your true self.

Debunking the Counselling Process

I think it is very important to be aware that this process of journeying into ourselves can be traumatic.

Often to uncover who we really are we need to revisit old wounds, so we can understand how we disconnected and why. We have patterns of 'being' in order to survive.

When we become disconnected, we don't know who we are and can become very lost and unhappy. We do not need to do this alone. There are many counsellors, therapists and mentors in the world who can hold a safe space for us to uncover and unpack our experiences and feelings.

Embarking on personal counselling or therapy, can be a frightening concept but can enable you to really begin to feel whole again; it's just about finding the right person. The right fit for you. Perhaps that's me? If so, my contact details are on the resources page.

AN INVITATION OF SELF-LOVE

Diamond dancer, what's the answer?
Always looking out yet not within.
Moving so fast not seeing what's in front of your own nose.

Stop a moment.
Breathe, listen, open your heart.
What is it you really seek?

What are you pushing against to fill the void within?
Look within dear friend, for what you seek does not lie outside.

You have all the answers within you.
Learn to trust yourself- love yourself.
Accept who you are.

You are beautiful.
There is no other like you.
You are a bright shining light, please stop extinguishing your flame.

Take fear by the hand, and love,
love wholly like you have never loved before.

Remember those dreams that stir deep within your soul.
Allow them to breathe, do not be conditioned by limits of other's
preconceptions of the truth.

Learn to live creatively, limitless.
Run freely beneath the open sky.
Let the rain cleanse you.

Let go, LET GO!

Connect with yourself again.
Find your own voice.
Open your heart to yourself.
"Become your own best friend".

INNER CALM
By
Jacquelina Wood-Haskuka

Sitting still
Breathing deep,
Silence, quiet
Peace to keep.

Quell the thoughts
Dissolve the pain,
Let the wave
Wash over you again.

For this is now
Not tomorrow,
Enjoy the moment
No more sorrow.

The Past awash in the crescent
Breathe to qualm,
Live in the present
Your inner calm.

What is inner calm and how do we find it? We often ask ourselves. The feeling of being at peace. The feeling of quiet content. In fact, the essence of happiness.

Smile and see how you feel as your cheeks rise up. That is a spark, an insight into that feeling of happiness and ultimately inner calm and peace.

Having a positive outlook, seeing that silver lining, being optimistic, always looking on the bright side of life, living in the now, can all help to keep us in the present moment, in that state of peace, of now.

Enjoy Happy Times, say, a walk in the fields with your dog and loved one, with the crisp air brushing against your cheeks, a picnic with your kids in the park on a warm hazy afternoon or a deep breath during a still, meditative moment at home, in the quiet of an early morning when the world is still sleeping.

Whilst cameras can capture these seconds to keep, share and remind us of happy times, taking a mental photo is just as good if not better at capturing that snapshot of a present moment, a moment we can retrieve whenever we are feeling low to bring us back to that happy state of now, of peace, of inner calm.

-End-

THE LOVE CHILD
By
Lady Jasmine Moorhouse
'Spirit Worker'

I was conceived out of wedlock on a hot summer's August evening on my Nan and Grandad's family farm.

My Dad being a couple of years older than my 20-year old Mum, fell in love with her grace and kind funny personality; her smile would light up any room she entered.

Four months after accidently getting pregnant with me, Mum and Dad married in a registry office on a cold December afternoon in 1976 in a small town in Somerset, although nothing is really accidental is it?!

Mum calls me her love child. x

I was born on a May morning, the 23rd to be precise, in 1977. I also know I was born very gifted and that realise now is the time to share my story with the world and hope whoever reads it will love my adventures with spirit and how I came to know them and work for the higher good.

The dog who nearly ate me!

Sat here nursing my 8-week old son, tears streaming down his face from a cold as a Mother and healer feel for him badly, I dread to think of my poor Mother all those years ago and how powerless and frightened she must have been.

You see, that day, my next door neighbour's dog took me as a 6-week newborn out of my pram and shook me like a rag doll on our front room floor (which was carpeted but solid concrete). I was lucky to escape with only cuts and bruises so our family doctor said, and hours later, the dog was put to sleep.

My childhood was quite difficult with the two boys next door as they possibly blamed me for taking their dog away forever. To this day I don't know how or why their dog attacked me.

Earth Angels

Do you believe in Earth Angels? I do, and some don't show up with wings and flying. I am of course referring to Angels born into human form to make a difference in the world. Some forget why they were sent until they are re-awakened on their true path. This happened to me although I wouldn't say I'm an Earth Angel - or maybe I am!

Along with so many others, I was opened up in traumatic and not so positive ways on many occasions. This I will share in the best way I can, prompted by my spirit guides who I know, know me better than I know myself.

In my story, things had presented themselves from age 8 through my teen-hood but I chose to ignore or wasn't really aware of my gift. It's best described as feeling uneasy around people or sensing things none of my friends understood, so I thought I wasn't normal or just very different, keeping things hidden and never speaking about it; too afraid I guess.

Human Skittles

Who likes to play human skittles? Not you I'm sure! But I was once one. I can laugh about it now, although at the time it wasn't fun at all but this was when I truly saw spirit.

I was an ordinary 8-year old playing out with friends on my estate; it was a hot summer but a week before, I pestered my parents for a pretty rainbow patch dress which I know my spirit family had some say in. Had they not, I definitely would not be here today playing skipping rope in the road with the teenagers.

I thought I was safe; everyone knew each other as it was and still is a very small village.

Happiness and laughter soon turned to screaming but I don't remember much or how far I was dragged up the road by, no not a car, but a motorbike! He was playing skittle Lorraine that day lol......

I was told by my Mum how lucky I was, as nurses fussed over me and a brain scan picked up damage to my frontal lobe - the biggest part of the brain - along with a fractured skull just above my left eye socket.

I remember what I now know to be an outer-body experience, switching from being in and out of consciousness. It was at this time that I saw my guide who I know as Mary.

She had beautiful long blonde hair which glistened like the sun with shimmering specks of gold highlights with an air of peace. I saw my little body carried up to my front door by my friends and teens and everything around me brighter in colour. My guide then told me it wasn't my time to go back! I just remember the awful pain, but I recovered quite quickly. I have chunks of my childhood I don't remember and when my friends ask do you remember this or that, I look at them quite dazed.

My Angel Tammy

Years went by and in my early teens I was bullied at school by boys in my year. I have no idea why, I just ignored it and did the best I could even through the toughest loss of one of my best friends.

Her name was Tammy and it was quite a shock when she crossed to the world of spirit, totally turning my world upside down. I named my 9-year old daughter after her and it took me two weeks to pluck up the courage to get the blessing from Tammy's Mum as I didn't want to offend anyone.

Tammy passed on the morning of the 5th Aug 1992. I felt uneasy that day and didn't know why. Then there was a knock at my front door. Three of my friends were standing there with tears flowing down their cheeks.

When I was told of her passing, an empty feeling came over me; sadness and disbelief but what followed will stay with me. I know the Angels came for my friend that morning and my kitchen was silent as a bright light came through the kitchen window and a voice saying, "It's ok". It felt like Sean out of the film Ghost and no word of a lie that theme song was played at Tammy's funeral, picked by my other best friend. Spirit intervention and the film plays around the time of Tammy's death most years.

I have to say it used to upset me but now I've made my peace and have more to tell of experiences I've had with tammy in spirit as she has worked with me and also came to me in a dream; during times I've been in hardship she's been there as she was in life.

There is a particular dream I will treasure always as I had been questioning my gifts and somewhat having big problems in my then marriage.

This was so vivid and beautiful; she had taken me to her graveside or I ended up there somehow, then she appeared as a beautiful winged Angel with wings white as snow stretched out asked me to come forward, put her arms and wings around me and said she would always be my friend and everything would be ok and to trust. I was doubting myself lots around that time with my spiritual work; I now know I really shouldn't.

I met my teen lover and future husband at the tender age of 17 when we partied harder than I should have. With holidays abroad, I lost touch with some friends, kept some and made other new friendships.

Dreams, Gifts & Family

At the age of 19 my Grandad passed to spirit; I was very close to him as a child and his passing wasn't a shock as knew he was very ill with bowel cancer two weeks before he went to spirit. I had a message saying he wouldn't have as long left as the Doctor had said two or more months. I remember telling my Dad who shrugged it off and told me the Doctors were right not me, but sure and sadly he passed not long after.

His funeral was lovely, but I was too frightened to go and see him in the Chapel of Rest so again, he came to me in a dream and took me there himself, dressed in a silk robe. When I spoke with my Mum, she told me that in fact he was dressed in his coffin in the very robes I had seen. I also know him to be around me a lot along with my Mum's Dad, who passed when she was 18.

I know my family members or a circle of them and was told I was gifted. My 91-year old Grandmother was one of them, my Mum and my Mum's Aunt who summoned me two weeks before she passed told me I was gifted and not to waste it. She did Tarot and tea leaves for years never letting on until she had to tell me. I guess that told me I was a chosen one but I didn't really know what she meant. Now I do bless her soul.

I think I've moved 6 times during my married life; Bristol being where we bought our first family home, and where I had our eldest son Ian who will be 16 in January 2018. Where has that time gone?!

The most traumatic time as I said earlier in my story was the night of 23rd April 2006 when my mum was taken ill suddenly, whilst I was heavily pregnant with my second son Kieran. I headed off down to Somerset, the very hospital I was born in. My Mum who was 50 suffered a life-changing stroke. The shock sent me into early labour and I didn't get the chance to see my Mum placed on life support; it was in the very early hours when I woke with labour pains.

What happened during my Son's birth scared me; I have no idea what actually happened, I just remember hearing my Mum's voice as I was out of it. Kieran's shoulders got stuck and I know my Husband was told to leave the room.

When I came to, 6 midwives were around the bed but no Husband; I felt comfortable knowing my mum would be ok as she had personally come to see me. It was later I was told she had in fact a 50/50 chance and had been resuscitated.

That was a big shock and led to my spiritual journey and working alongside spirit when some 6-weeks after the birth of Kieran, my Sister's boyfriend was involved in a motorbike accident where he had not been wearing a helmet and been showing off on a more powerful bike than he could handle.

He was air lifted to Frenchay Hospital Bristol and was in an induced coma. My mum had by this time pulled out of her stroke but was left paralysed down one side of her body and had months of recovery. She is to this day a very strong woman and so loving. As for my Sister, with myself having just given birth and taking on more than I could handle, this is when I was thrown in the deep end literally and spiritually.

Hello Spirit World

I was visiting the hospital with my Sister, seeing her boyfriend's lifeless body, just as Mum had been, and I really opened up to the spirit world to the point where I thought I was going mad!

I was hearing voices somewhere; it was not a very nice experience but having family and friends in spirit, prompted me to get help as it was becoming out of hand. So I looked in the Yellow Pages and not knowing a thing about it, phoned a Medium called Bernie Scott. She worked with me for what seemed like a year 1:1, to clear the negativity around me and also to give me the healing I needed as my chakras were out of synch.

This is where, although at the time I was scared, it changed who I was and I became spiritually aware with no going back.

Another friend Chrissy had confided in me as she knew I was spiritually aware but I didn't truly believe it.

She just said I needed to prove it and that I may have my chance one day. What she said put a cold shiver down my spine and sure enough it came true.

She had told me she would pass to spirit but didn't know how. She was pregnant at the time and months went by. She had her baby boy then became ill with Type-3 Strep. She had gone through so much as it spread through from her womb and she'd had to have both feet amputated.

I know she asked to see me before she passed to spirit but she'd already died before I could reach the hospital, leaving 4 beautiful children behind. Over the next few months, I knew she was around me and I was even able to give her ex a message that he would meet someone. I know from what he had told me that he knows she's around them. I've lost touch with them as it spooked them out not being ready for it I also know my friend's youngest daughter to be gifted.

Over the course of a couple of years, right up to the time I moved with my two boys and my (now ex) Husband to Trowbridge, I practiced in a spiritual circle group run by Bernie and did my Reiki 1 with her. I then wanted to push myself more but had to find another Circle Development Group in Westbury. I attended this Group and got my Diploma 1 in Mediumship then went on to do my Reiki 2.

I regularly send out distant healing and give my mum healing. I have had a couple of clients and done readings for the military families in both Warminster and Salisbury plain, along with party bookings. I am also learning more and plan to open my own healing room and to eventually do this from home as I divorced in March 2017.

After 20 years, of this, I know that life can be so hard for me and so many other spiritually aware Earth Angels. It's very sensitive work which won't be over until we ourselves pass to spirit. But I also know that as Spirit, we take what we learn here so to speak, as this is a continued adventure whether on the earth plain or in the spirit realm.

A lot of love is needed in this world, positive thinking and kindness for future generations and to look after what we have for tomorrow relies on what we all do today. Good deeds don't go unanswered and spreading love rather than hate as the world goes around so does lifebirth and deathbirth both mirror each other.

I have always believed in reincarnation; I also know good and bad light and dark exist as part of life. A flower needs darkness to bloom into beauty when light hits the soil just as growth is required in each and every one of us. I also believe we have our own destiny; we choose the path to take, helped by our guides if we willing to listen. And yes I admit I had been stubborn and made wrong choices when I did not listen to my guides. I messed up, took chances and then wished I had gone with my gut... ummm how many can relate here?

Well I'm coming to the end of my story now, but wish everyone who reads this, love and light.

Oh, and I bet some are wondering why I don't use my real name as my business name. There's a good explanation for this; I asked spirit what they thought would be a good name for me and they gave me Lady Jasmine.

I never really liked my name. I remember my Mum saying I could change it when I'm older then she asked why that name in particular. My reply was that Spirit see me as a delicate flower, sweet but with a strong routed growth, just like Jasmine.

As far as I know I'm not royalty lol. Maybe I am in spirit! So, to avoid causing my clients any confusion, I have bought myself a plot of land in a Manor which gives me my title Lady Jasmine Moorhouse, spiritual medium and reiki healer.

Many thanks.

Sincerely,
Spirit Worker Lady Jasmine

MY CHAKRA JOURNEY OF DEEP HEALING AND TRANSFORMATION
By
Carol Boyes

Dear reader, please allow me to introduce myself. My name is Carol and I live in Witney Oxfordshire just a stone's throw away from the beautiful Cotswolds. I am a single Mum with two grown up sons from my first marriage (both in their 30's) and my 17-year old daughter from my second marriage (It's just her and I at home now).

May I first say how deeply honoured I feel to be part of this truly wonderful anthology with many of my soul sisters from the Discover your Purpose Facebook group who have all played their part in making this book come alive. It is my belief that it is no coincidence that this book has found its way to you, and my prayer is that you find exactly what you need from the pages within.

My part in this, is to tell you a little bit about my story, from where it all began to more recently as I embarked on a journey of discovery, deep healing and transformation. May I just say here to avoid any confusion that yes, my story begins in the middle, jumps forward to the present, then reverts to the past, before returning again to the now. This is not a mistake, it is how I can best explain how I came to be where I am today.

Let me first go back to the year 2000. A year of mixed emotions and a year that sparked something within me that I was not expecting. My dear Mum Geraldine (Gaye to her family and friends) passed away on the 30th January after many months of ill health. She was the dearest, kindest, most loving and patient lady I have ever known. My world was rocked beyond belief and this was made worse because I was carrying the granddaughter she would never get to meet. My heart was breaking with sadness, yet I so wanted it to be filled with joy for the little girl I carried.

My beautiful daughter Cortney was born on the 24th April 2000 and the minute I held her in my arms I loved her so deeply and somehow I knew my Mum was close. I felt her with me and I felt comforted. From that day on I knew I had to learn more about the spirit world. So, this was when my journey into the unknown began. I was searching for answers. Where had she gone? Was she ok? Was she at peace? Was she with my other family members who had gone before her? So many questions going round and round in my head.

I began to read books about the spirit world, I went to Spiritualist churches, mediumship demonstrations, watched TV programmes and whatever else I could to find the answers I was searching for. I joined a closed development circle through my local Spiritualist church in 2010 and it was from here that I embarked upon many different things such as mediumship and spiritual healing. I became passionate about all things Angels. They really spoke to me and I felt a connection, so I studied and gained my qualification as a certified Angel card reader and Angelic healing practitioner.

I finally began to feel that I had found my calling and that this was indeed where my soul felt at home. It was during this time of learning and discovery that I was able to find some of the answers I had been searching for regarding my dear Mum and I felt at peace in the knowledge that she was indeed safe, whole and healed once more and I finally knew that she was and always will be, just a thought away.

In 2013, I came to realise that things between my second husband and I were no longer going in the right direction. My spiritual path was calling to me so deeply and I felt my heart needed to follow, and whilst to a degree he was supportive of this, I knew deep down that our relationship was indeed drifting beyond repair. So, in October 2013 we parted ways and he left the family home. This was when my life truly began to change.

I was now a single Mum again with a 13-year old daughter to take care of and I was determined that I would give us both the best possible life I could.

As a self-employed cleaner, I took care of two large holiday homes for one of my clients. This kept me super busy, it was tiring and I didn't enjoy it at all. It was definitely not what I wanted to do long term, however it was supporting me, paying the bills and providing for my daughter and I.

My passion and my long-term dream was to build my own heart centred healing business, and to help others on their own healing journeys. So, alongside my cleaning and housekeeping jobs, running the home, taking care of my daughter (who at this time in her life was suffering with severe anxiety which led to depression) I also became a Nana when my son and daughter-in-law blessed our family with a beautiful baby girl.

Somehow, I managed to find the time to embark on further studies between 2013 and 2016 and proudly gained my qualifications in Reiki levels 1 & 2. I studied Tarot and gained a diploma in Aromatherapy massage and qualified as a Chakra balance practitioner. Little did I know that this last qualification was going to play such a huge part of my healing journey going forward.

Out with the old and in with the new: December 2016.
The end of the year brought a huge and unexpected shock! I was still doing my cleaning and housekeeping jobs as they were my main source of income. Then one day around the middle of December, quite out of the blue, I received a call from the lady who's holiday homes I had taken care of for the past 10 years. She had decided that she was no longer taking any bookings with immediate effect and was putting the properties up for sale on the market. She had no mortgage to worry about, so this was to be her retirement fund and she was off the travel the world!

Whilst I was happy for her, I was terrified for myself and my daughter. This was going to affect my income drastically and I immediately went into panic and survival mode. What was I going to do? How would I pay my bills? Would I be able to meet all my financial commitments?

I felt so much fear around how I would manage. It was at this point I knew I had to take a leap of faith. And leap I did.

January 2017 I stepped wholeheartedly into my heart centred business. I began offering all of my services to clients from my home and I booked myself into Mind Body and Spirit fairs where I offered intuitive guidance readings and healing treatments. I was amazed at how quickly things seemed to fall into place and the bookings continued through the year. I began to get regular clients coming for healing treatments and for guidance and coaching readings and my little business began to blossom. All seemed well in my world, but I was about to learn again just how quickly things can change.

June 2017 everything that could go wrong began to go wrong, and it all seemed to come at once. It was a dark time and I found myself being drawn back to the past. Memories coming up that I thought I had dealt with and let go of came back to haunt me. Only this time the pain was deeper than before. I wasn't coping and my health began to suffer. I remember feeling as if something was brewing but I just didn't know what.

Everything seemed to be crashing around me. Clients were cancelling, events were being cancelled or I had to pull out for one reason or another.

Once again I felt myself begin to panic, I was losing income and my survival mode kicked in again and I began to look for more cleaning work, even though this meant going backwards. I felt it was my only option. It was at this point that I found myself being deeply guided towards working with my Chakra energy centres. And I'm so grateful that I listened.

The synchronistic events that happened next, meant that I found myself working with a Chakra mentor who helped me to increase my knowledge and take to the next level all that I had previously learnt in my Chakra balance studies. This later proved to be pivotal in my healing journey.

I began to pay attention to my intuition and what it was trying to tell me, and I began working deeply with each Chakra one by one from Root to Crown. This is when I truly understood on a whole new level the power these amazing energy centres have and how much they can help us to heal. This was more than just the Chakra balancing with crystals that I had been taught initially, this was deep deep healing on all levels. Physically, emotionally, mentally and spiritually.

I meditated every day with each Chakra and I opened myself up to receive the messages each one held for me. I journaled upon my findings and I discovered I had so much pain, guilt, shame, fear, self limiting beliefs and even ancestral energy deeply held within each Chakra, and all of this had created so many blocks that had, and still were showing up for me, not just in my physical world, but with my health too.

It was during these Chakra healing meditations that I was to uncover some deep-seated memories from my past of the abuse I went through at the hands of my first Husband way back in the late 70's early 80's. The memories came flooding back and they hit hard! I was right back there feeling the pain, the fear, the shame of not standing up for myself and for not protecting my two little boys who witnessed far too much as their Father abused me.

I felt disgust and guilt towards myself because I was afraid to grab my boys and run. I hated myself and I hated the Mother I was back then. I felt to blame and I began to berate myself all over again. I should have fought back. I should have told someone. I should have taken my boys and left. Instead I allowed the abuse to continue for 7 long years, before in 1986 I finally found the courage from somewhere to take my boys and leave.

Sadly it wasn't quite over and during the early days after we left he stalked and spied on us, made threatening calls to me and my family, and then after making one last attempt at taking my life with a knife at my throat, he finally gave up and left us alone.

So, here I was 31 years later about to embark on a healing journey that was not going to be an easy one, but one I knew I had to take, all of this was coming up for a reason and I needed to understand why. For years I thought I had dealt with it. It wasn't affecting me, I wasn't thinking about, so I must have dealt with it right? Wrong!

Here it was, all that emotion, all that pain, all that fear. Everything that I had buried for so many years was erupting like a volcano, spewing out from the depths of my being. I felt broken. I felt ashamed. I felt completely violated all over again. All this had been festering away beneath the surface all this time. I couldn't understand, why now? Why after all these years was this pain revealing itself so strongly. I was soon to find out.

The answer revealed itself: July 2017.
A month had passed on my Chakra healing journey, and I was discovering the answers to many of my self-limiting beliefs. I learned that so many of the issues I'd had in my life, actually came from the abuse I had suffered and that it was in fact the energy of these memories that had been held and hidden in my Chakras all these years. This had shown up many, many times in my life as lack of confidence, low self-esteem, fear, self-loathing, low self-worth and at one point, I had even developed a stutter because of the fear of saying the wrong thing and being torn to pieces verbally or getting yet another slap because of it.

This is why I created the belief that it was safer to just keep my mouth shut and to not say anything. I now know this was also where my fear of public speaking stemmed from, because I had never been allowed to have an opinion, so I just kept quiet for fear of saying the wrong thing and upsetting anyone.

Whilst this was a painful process, it was at the same time liberating because I finally truly felt I was on the way to healing and letting go of the pain and self-limiting beliefs I had carried for so long. I still didn't have the answer as to why all this had come up now.

It was the middle of July when I got a call from my first Husband's Brother (with whom I had always remained friends, although we rarely had any contact) to tell me that my ex Father-in-Law had passed away. He said that myself and the boys were more than welcome to attend the funeral, but of course it meant that HE would also be there.

We spoke for some time on the phone, and I told him I would need to discuss it with my boys. However, I already knew that I myself wanted to go. After all, I had always gotten along with my Father-in-Law, he had always been kind to me and I wanted to pay my respects. I had always felt that he had been deeply ashamed by his son's behaviour, although we never spoke about HIM during any of the times we met.

My eldest Son decided not to go, my younger Son decided he wanted to and I respected both their decisions equally. So, the decision was made and the day of the funeral arrived.

I finally understood why just over a month before everything from my past had reared its ugly head. I truly believe that spirit had stepped in, paved the way and prepared me for the day that I would come face to face after 30 years with the man who had abused me and left me feeling unworthy of anything for so long. And because of the healing journey through the Chakras I had just embarked on, I was able to hold my head high with dignity, pride and respect in myself in the knowledge that everything I had been feeling about myself was not true, but purely how HE had made me feel.

I was and I am a woman of confidence. I was and I am a woman whose voice is important. I was and I am woman who is worthy of love, kindness and respect. I was always all of these things. I had just forgotten who I was because of the fear HE made me feel. I finally understood that all those self-limiting beliefs, fears and anxieties that I had carried within me for so many years, were the energetic memory of the emotions of how HE had made me feel about myself. He was of course simply the catalyst!

I began to feel that the real me was finally being set free from the cords of attachment to so many untruths. You see the thing is this: as humans we tend to look outside of ourselves for answers. We need reassurance and for someone to tell us what to do, or that things will be okay. We look for someone to fix us. We go to the GP when we are feeling low, or sad or in pain, and all too often we are given a magic pill and told to go away and take it and that it will make us feel better.

Whilst yes of course there are genuine times when we need medication to help us get better, no amount of medication will help if the problem is an energetic one. So, the truth is sadly that all too often the magic pill only masks the symptoms, without getting to the real cause of the pain. All too often we get told to pull ourselves together, or to pick ourselves up and get on with it, or not to let things bother us! So what do we do then? We shove all the emotions we may be feeling down so deep, all the pain, the sadness, the shame, the guilt, the fear all stuffed down, where we think it won't affect us anymore, and there it sits, our ticking time bomb, waiting for the day when you least expect it to blow up in our faces and boy oh boy did I learn that first hand.

Time to say goodbye.
The day of the funeral came, and whilst yes it felt rather surreal, I had never felt more confident in my life than I did when I walked right up to him after the service and gave my sincere condolences for his loss, and then out of nowhere, I found myself saying that I felt sorry for him, that I didn't hold any bitterness or hate towards him.

I told him that I felt sorry for him because he had never been man enough to be a Father to his children or a Husband to his Wife. I told him that to be a Father and a Husband, it requires the ability to love and sadly that was something he was clearly incapable of. Then I wished him well, and before he could speak I turned and walked away. It truly was time to say goodbye.

No more would I allow the energetic memory of the past to cause me any more pain.

As I look back now, I truly believe that Spirit knew that I needed the down time from my work so as to focus on my own healing journey and prepare for the challenge that I was about to face. Which is why I believe clients were cancelling and events were too. Spirit knew I needed to heal and that Is why I was guided towards working with my Chakras because they held the key.

My Chakra energy system had been holding the energy of the memories of all the pain, guilt, shame and fear from the abuse and I needed to go back to that in order to understand how it had been playing out and showing up my whole life!

By going within and doing the work, trusting my intuition and feeling into what came up for me, acknowledging and owning it instead of brushing it under the carpet and pretending it had happened to someone else, the way I had done for so many years. I found that day by day, little by little, I began to feel more confident, less afraid, more self-assured and more powerful than I had done in a very long time.

I discovered something so powerful and it fuels me every day. I came to realise that It is because of everything I went through, not in spite of it, that I am who I am today. I finally realised that, all of those negative emotions, all of that pain and fear, all of those times I felt not good enough, not worthy enough, not lovable enough, do not define who I am. I am all that I am because of all that I went through.

And I can now show gratitude for this because it has helped me to understand exactly what my purpose is. My purpose, I believe is to help as many beautiful souls out there as I can find their true authentic selves once more. To step out of fear and to step into love. To let go of self-limiting beliefs and to step into their power. To walk once more with heads held high and to be able to say. I am who I am. I am not what you dictate I should be.

And back to the now: October 2017.
To say the last few months have been intense would probably be an understatement!

But, I hold my hand on my heart when I say this, without going through this whole experience I wouldn't be doing what I'm doing now.

Because of my own experience and by going through this Chakra healing journey myself, I can speak with truth about the benefits of Chakra energy work and the healing it can bring. It is because of this that I felt inspired to help others to do the same.

I am deeply passionate about the power of Chakra energy healing, which is why I created my 8-week online Chakra Bootcamp programme where I teach and guide those who feel inspired to work with me on their own healing journey using the same techniques that I used to heal myself. I feel truly blessed that because of my own personal experiences, I am able to offer my support and guidance, and be a part of someone else's healing journey of discovery and transformation. Chakra energy healing changed my life for the better, and if I may be of service and help you to change yours, I would be deeply honoured to do so. From my heart to yours. Namaste.

-End-

MY WOMB STORY
By
Carol Boyes

It's dark in here, like an undiscovered cave. I enter slowly, carefully.
I've been here before I'm sure of it!
It feels familiar yet why is it so dark?
Wait what's that I see? Is that a light? So tiny so small?
I breathe and I go in deeper, my skin feels damp with trepidation as I
enter this deep dark cave that I feel sure was once filled with light.

My breathing deepens as I whisper "Hello old friend".
In the silence I sense a stirring, something is awakening....
My heart pounds in my chest as I wait .... and then she speaks.
"You're back....I have missed you so."

I feel such emotion within me as I feel her love and her pain mingling
and blending as it swirls within the depths of her beauty.
I have come home and she has welcomed me back without judgment
and with such unconditional love that my heart swells with gratitude
for her acceptance.

And now the healing comes....
with tears of joy I let go one by one...
I'm sorry, please forgive me, I love you, thank you.
Over and over and over.

And now peace comes...
The light returns and the beauty I behold is beyond expression. So
many colours fill the space that was once so dark as she awakens in
all her glory once more from the neglect that I had imposed upon
her.

But no more, no more will I take for granted this sacred space, no
more will I allow her to be abused, mistreated and ignored...
I hear you old friend and I am ready to listen.

My beautiful Womb I love you.

*"Always remember that you do not need to
explain yourself or prove
anything to anyone.*

*If they cannot accept you for you – then it is time
to move on."*

Cath B

PICTURE YOURSELF IN A BOAT ON A RIVER
By
Edna Clark

These are the words to a very popular song. We wonder where the thoughts came from for the writer to put these words together and add music.

Whenever we consciously write anything, any words of wisdom or letter to a friend, we tune into a consciousness that allows the words to flow smoothly and the repetition of this is never completely free from the love and possibility that we are being helped.

Pen and paper, words and song follow each other. If you can allow this to take place by taking your own mind and letting it take a short rest, while your body writes words of wisdom, love, honesty, prophecy then this is a truly wonderful thing.

Sometimes as a human being we can become so full of ego, so full of self-righteousness that we think it unthinkable to allow the words to be written without checking, re-writing and changing our original writing.

When we are in tune and act for the greater good of all, nothing can compare to the speed and acceptance of the writing that follows.

Within us all, we have the answer to every question within us all is the bright light of spirit, the essence of all that is and ever will be.

This bright light holds wisdom, connection to the high realms, our ancestors, shamans, tribal folk, celts, the underworld, the animal kingdom and the list is endless.

It is said we have a heart mind, I am inclined to believe this, for as I write this short message, my mind keeps trying to take the lead, then my writing falters and I am unsure.

When I am able to keep the mind out, there are no breaks, simply flow and connection to the other side, the other world that we can access whenever we ask. Ask spirit gently to work with you, this is such an enjoyable process, you will wonder why you had not tried it before.

It is fast, it is truth, it is love, it is satisfaction.

It is connection to the unseen, the limitless help we can call upon at any time from our spirit friends who love us, and love to communicate with and through us.

When you feel the connection has ended, always say thank you for coming, please come again.........xx

-End-

THE GIFT OF LIFE
by
Amanda Thomas

My story of surviving childhood sexual abuse and battling infertility to become a Mother.

Before I talk about my own healing journey, I want to begin by saying that wherever you are in your life right now and whatever storm you are fighting, you are not alone. You are not alone because there are countless others just like you, struggling in silence to live each day, to keep their head above deep waters of pain, grief and fear and simply exist in the world. You may be feeling that it's just you, that there's something wrong with you, that you were just destined for a life of bad luck, pain and loss and you just aren't meant to be happy, healthy or wealthy. But I want to take you in my arms and hold you and tell you that

I have felt this way too and it doesn't have to feel like that because none of that is true. You are not alone. You are loved. You are enough. You are worthy of a life filled with happiness and love. You matter and the world is a more beautiful place for having you in it. I have lived down the deepest darkest well, imprisoned in a cell, suffocated by grief and pain, shackled by fear, conformity and negative self-beliefs. There have been numerous occasions when suicide has crossed my mind and self-harm both physical and psychological, have ripped at my flesh and mind like the teeth of a lion through its prey. I have lived and experienced intensely dark times but I have also witnessed the magnificent light that follows. The most ferocious of storms have engulfed me and literally had me on my knees ready to give up but it is those moments, when I have been able to summon one last ounce of strength, that have been followed by miracles, illuminated in glorious light and the most serene calmness and profound joy. They say that the darkest part of the night is just before the dawn and just when you're ready to give up, the miracle is just around the corner and I now know both these things to be true.

I know it might not feel like it right now but you are a powerful being of light with incredible potential and you have everything you need within you to find your rainbow and live the life you dream of. We are all pilgrims, trying to find our way home, back home to a place long forgotten; our beautiful authentic self. So when that darkness grips you remember this...the caterpillar had no idea that when he entered that dark chrysalis that it would emerge the most beautiful butterfly, gifted with wings to soar above the world, full of wisdom from its courageous journey.

This is my story of hope, strength, self-preservation, being an adult survivor of childhood sexual abuse and battling infertility to become a Mother. It's the pilgrimage I took in order to find myself, through sheer grit and determination, hard work and self-healing. I hope that by sharing my story, it will give hope to others and be a source of inspiration for personal healing and to never give up on your dreams.

Life is a beautiful and miraculous gift but I have to admit, I haven't always felt that way. For as long as I can remember, life has been one continuous battle and I have had to cling on by my fingernails, with every ounce of my being, in order to function and exist in the world. To the world I seemed perfectly together, a swan gracefully gliding across the water. Yet my external world was not a true reflection of my turbulent inner world. Inside I faced a daily fight for survival, a daily struggle to keep the multiple layers of trauma that had been buried, contained within the walls that I had built. Fatigue, stress, overwhelm and chronic illness were a constant battle, born out of unresolved trauma, suppressed emotions and the desperation to cling on to life and just be in the world. For most of my life, the darkness was thick and heavy and I was constantly on the brink of being sucked up by the tornado that raged outside my door. Consumed by the pain of my past and terrified by fear about my future, I was paralysed by shame and tortured by periods of anxiety and depression. Sometimes both at once, other times I'd yo-yo between the two, in a cruel game of tug of war.

It's hard sometimes to put in to words what we are feeling and experiencing because there just aren't any adequate words to describe such debilitating pain and sadness. Most of my life I have pushed down my feelings and emotions, refusing to acknowledge their existence; to sustain that is truly exhausting. I often wonder how I'm still here, how I have survived the things I have had to endure. Yet here I am, on the surface a 'normal' woman. Despite all the pain, all the suffering, all the loss, all the turmoil, I have found a way to survive and though for the majority of my life I have been dissociated from myself, I have always had a lot of empathy for others and a strong sense of wanting to help and support people. I guess that's been a way of avoiding how I was truly feeling and I noticed that often what I gave to others, is exactly what I needed myself. My pain and grief were like the ground beneath my feet; layer upon layer, upon layer of unresolved emotions and suppressed grief; a dark swirling, powerful tornado, caged like a wild beast of the night. At times, that tornado had a glimpse of freedom and it took every ounce of strength that I had, to cling on and not get swept away and consumed by its dark storm.

My raging tornado mainly consisted of two particularly traumatic events: a stolen childhood through the violation of my vulnerable seven-year-old body and the loss of my womanhood and the sacred gift of motherhood because of a rare congenital syndrome. So many choices taken away, so much shame, so much sadness, so much loss and a heart and soul fractured by pain and grief. Yet despite it all, there has always been a tiny spark of light deep inside me, willing me to keep going and not give up on life; giving me the strength to keep treading water and keep my head up, to stop the water from pouring in to my mouth and nose, flooding my lungs and starving me of my last breath.

At around the age of 7, I was sexually abused by someone I knew. My fragile, innocent body touched and violated by an adult, the people as children, we look up to and trust to care for us. As it happened, I froze like a rabbit in headlights, too petrified to move. The sheer panic and fear is hard to put into words; I was absolutely terrified and knew what was happening was very wrong but I was frozen to the spot, unable to move my body to run away or open my mouth to scream, as I was doing so inside my head.

A piece of my soul left my body that day and drifted away; unable to cope with the pain and emotional distress of what was happening. It left me feeling disgustingly dirty, so ashamed, so afraid and I felt that somehow it had been my fault. I changed in that moment, from an outgoing little girl full of playful mischief to a terrified, introverted and lonely child. I couldn't sleep on my own from that point because I was petrified that he would come for me in the night. Being alone and night times were the worst, as they brought terror, nightmares and whispering voices inside my head. My parents had no idea what had caused this sudden and drastic change in my behavior. I wish I'd been able to tell them what had happened to me, so that they understood but I couldn't bring myself to say it, I didn't know how to because I was filled with so much shame. As time passed it became harder and harder and so I simply said nothing.

Years passed and I was plagued with flashbacks and nightmares until one day at senior school when I was 15, I stayed behind after registration and blurted out the sexual abuse to my Tutor. I needed to speak out about what had happened to me because it was tearing me apart. My tutor was amazing and listened to me with empathy and without judgement. He informed me that he had a duty to inform the Head and he would then need to inform Social Services. I knew in that moment that I would have to tell my Parents but I just didn't know how I was going to. I decided that the only way I could, would be to write a letter to them both because I knew I wouldn't be able to physically speak the words.

 A week or two later, after I spoke out, I was asked to go to the local Social Services department and my Dad attended with me. It was utterly heartbreaking and soul destroying having to go over what had happened to me in detail, in front of my Dad. I was so ashamed. I can't imagine what listening to that must have felt like for my Dad. I also spoke to a female Police Officer, who informed me that as several years had passed it would be very difficult to prove and it would be my word against his. She said that they could go and speak to him but that all he would get would be a slap on the wrists. A slap on the wrists?! How could that be, when I was left with a life-long scar, nightmares, shame, shattered self-esteem and no self-confidence? How could someone be able to get away with such a cruel, despicable act of violation to a young child and get away with nothing but a slap on the wrists?! Discouraged by this, I decided to leave it and take no further action, which was a decision that later in life I came to regret and has caused me further anguish and guilt.

I have always worried that there may have been others too and felt that if I had had the strength and support to take action, then maybe I could have prevented someone else from suffering the same fate as me.

I was referred to the NSPCC for counselling, where I attended for a few months. My counsellor helped me to see that it was in no way my fault, I had done nothing to cause what had happened to me and so a little of the shame I felt lifted. I had developed some obsessive behaviours following the years after the abuse and one of them was counting when I washed myself. I would count so that I washed equally on each side and if I lost count, I would start all over again. I guess this was because I never felt clean and it gave me an element of control over parts of my life.

There are times even now when I drive past where it happened, or my husband touches me in a certain way and it all comes flooding back. My body freezes and sheer panic takes over. Rather than being consumed by this, I now handle those moments by acknowledging the feelings and emotion and the way it feels in my body, taking a deep breath and then letting it go. There are days when this is harder than others but for the most part now, I acknowledge the memory and the associated feeling and emotions and let them come and go, like visitors. Being able to deal with this in this way is because of the healing journey I have been on and am still on.

Not long after I had spoken out about the abuse, I started experiencing excruciating abdominal pain and there was still no sign of my periods, despite the rest of my body starting to show signs of puberty at around the age of 9 or 10. I had been back and forth to the doctors on several occasions, until finally one GP referred me to a Gynecologist who examined me and advised that I would need to have a Laparoscopy to investigate; a procedure done under general anesthetic to place a tiny telescope through the belly button to look inside.

The day I went in for the Laparoscopy, is a day I will never forget. My whole world came crashing down around me. As I sat on the hospital bed recovering, a nurse came and informed me that my Consultant would like to see me in his consultation room downstairs. I instantly knew that the news was not going to be good because he would have come to see me at the bedside ordinarily. As I got dressed, thoughts raced inside head and my heart pounded in my chest. I don't think anything could have prepared me for what the Consultant told me, as I sat in front of him with my parents beside me. He told me that I had a rare congenital disorder called Rokitansky Syndrome, which some years later, I found out was formally known as MRKH Syndrome (Mayer Rokitansky Kuster Hauser). He told me that I didn't have a womb and would therefore never be able to have children because I couldn't become pregnant, couldn't carry or give birth to a baby. I just sat there in silence, unable to take it all in. The Consultant confirmed that I had both ovaries and fallopian tubes but my right ovary had a Dermoid Cyst on it, which would need to be removed. A dermoid cyst is an abnormal growth and can be made up of hair, teeth, fluid or skin glands. Great, I thought! So I'm not capable of growing my own womb but I can grow a bloody extra-terrestrial quite successfully!

If that wasn't enough of a blow, he then went on to tell me that my vagina was also undeveloped but that there were options to resolve this. I didn't hear everything he said because I drifted off somewhere trying desperately to process what I'd just been told. I lost another piece of my soul that day, as it drifted off someplace, the reality of the present was just too much for me, too painful, too devastating. I wanted desperately to just run out of that room. I wished that my Parents hadn't been there with me and I couldn't bring myself to look at them. I willed myself not to cry, not to break down, not to scream. Instead I just stared into space, in utter shock.

The Consultant obviously saw the shock and despair on my face and said that I "probably just wanted to get out of there" and so he would arrange to see me again to go over things in more detail.

I don't think I said a word as we left that room and walked from the hospital to the car. I didn't speak during the journey home and just stared out of the window the entire way. I'm not entirely sure when I spoke again. I felt overwhelming embarrassment, shame, despair, guilt, sadness and utter heartbreak. I had nightmares about being called a freak and this haunted me during my waking hours. I kept thinking it must be some mistake and expected the phone to ring and for someone to tell me that they'd made a mistake and got the wrong patient. All that kept running through my mind was that no man would ever want me or love me. I couldn't see a future and I had no idea how I was going to live in the world. I also felt guilty and such a let-down that I'd never make my Parents Grandparents. I felt such a disappointment, an utter failure, so much shame and so unworthy of being a woman; deprived of the sacred space to be able to bring a new life in to the world.

I returned to the hospital to discuss the various treatment options to develop my vagina and originally I had opted to go in for surgery with balloon therapy. It involved an operation to take a skin graft from my inner thigh to develop a vagina surgically, followed by weeks in hospital, whilst a balloon was gradually inflated inside me daily; extremely invasive and hugely personal. The other option was Dilator Therapy, a daily process of pushing a dilator against the existing vaginal tissue to stretch it over time. Neither option appealed to me but I knew I had to choose one, if I wanted to experience a normal sex life. As my surgery date loomed ever closer, niggling doubts crept in and I began to doubt my choice. I couldn't face the thought of the surgery and the thought of having a balloon inside me being inflated by someone, was just horrific, so I called the hospital and told them I had changed my mind and wanted to try dilator therapy instead. I started seeing a Nurse Specialist and using the dilators. It was so humiliating and so painful to begin with. I hated doing it, it felt so clinical and the only way I found it possible to do it, was to dissociate from my body. I received very little if any, real psychological support, other than talking to the Nurse Specialist following my diagnosis and it has only been in the last 10 years that I have realised just how much I needed psychological support. I was a young teenager at a significant point in my life at puberty, when hormones are raging and the body is changing from a girl to a young woman. To be dealt such devastating and life changing news at that stage of my life had a huge impact on every part of me and who I was.

I had always known I wanted to have children one day and had been maternal from a young age. Like many young women I dreamt of getting married and having a beautiful family; that was all I ever wanted. I wasn't particularly career driven, I just wanted to be a wife and a Mother and yet there I was thinking that I would never be either. The loss of this is so hard to put into words. I felt so empty and incomplete. To look at me you'd never know there was anything wrong. I have lived most my life since my diagnosis of MRKH, feeling so different to every female I know. Feeling like I don't fit in, that I'm damaged, incomplete and broken. I criticised and berated myself daily because I felt so let down by my body. The things that I have said to myself and the way in which I said them, have been so cruel, so unfair and I would never speak to another human being in that way, so why did I do that to myself?

In 2004 I met my Husband and around 6 months in to our relationship, I knew I had to tell him that I couldn't have children because my feelings were very different for him than I'd experienced in any relationship before him. I was terrified he'd finish with me but instead, he said the best thing that he could have said, "I love you for you, not whether you can give me children or not". So you see, Prince Charmings really do exist and I married mine in 2011.

My complex health journey didn't end there and I was also diagnosed with Polycystic Ovarian Syndrome, a Pituitary Tumour, which I first had to have biannual and then annual MRI's to monitor. Thankfully the tumour didn't require any further treatment, as it shrunk of its own accord. Then in 2006 I underwent a second Laparoscopy with key-hole surgery, following a year of debilitating right sided abdominal pain. I was told I had Endometriosis and had to have my right ovary and fallopian tube removed because the adhesions had stuck them to my bowel and the damage was irreparable. Another cruel blow; how could someone without a womb have Endometriosis? Thankfully my bowel was undamaged but I felt my femininity slipping away, bit by bit. Then in 2011, a month before I got married, I had a third Laparoscopy with key-hole surgery and had my left fallopian tube removed. They saved my left ovary, which remains stitched in its rightful place and I fondly refer to it as my warrior ovary. I was incredibly grateful to have my left ovary and this became even more significant when my Husband and I found out about IVF Surrogacy.

Hoping desperately to become a family, my Husband and I visited our GP and were referred to an IVF clinic in Wales, where we were living at the time and not long after we got married, a friend blew us away, when she offered to be our surrogate. There are two types of Surrogacy; Straight where the surrogates own egg is used and Gestational where an embryo is created through the process of IVF, using the Intended Mother's egg and the Intended Father's sperm and then an embryo is implanted in to the surrogate. Because I had an ovary and produced eggs, we opted for Gestational Surrogacy, to have a chance of having our own biological child.

Our journey was a bumpy road and it pushed me to my upper limits of being able to cope. After two years of being on the waiting list and a week before we were due to start treatment, we were told that the clinic could no longer offer us treatment and was being closed down. We were absolutely devastated but after appealing to IVF Wales, we were able to keep our funding and decided to move back to Wiltshire to be closer to our family and found a local clinic, where we started treatment. Unfortunately, it just wasn't meant to be and we went through two failed cycles and then made the decision to not make any further attempts as a team. The whole process put an immense strain on my relationship with my friend and I struggled to cope with the intense emotions and loss and I began self-harming in the form of cutting myself.

Shocked and terrified by this, I immediately sought the support of my GP. I'd all but given up on being a Mother at this point because I just didn't feel that I had the strength to continue with IVF Surrogacy. But that's when the first of my biggest miracles happened.

After giving myself around 6 months to grieve and pick myself back up, I mustered all my strength and we became what's known as 'Active' Intended Parents with Surrogacy UK, an organisation whose ethos is friendship first, an ethos that appealed greatly to us.

We were incredibly lucky and it didn't take long before we were getting to know a wonderful lady and her family and after 3 months, she confirmed that she'd like to work with us and we were absolutely over the moon when we became pregnant first time after a frozen cycle. There are no words to describe the joy and elation we felt. No words to describe the unconditional love we felt towards our baby and the amazing lady that was supporting us to achieve our dream. The day our son was born was the happiest day of our life, at last we were a family of three. There I was holding my son in my arms, his little hand curled around my finger and his dark brown eyes looking deep in to my soul.

Becoming a Mother was everything I had imagined it to be and more. Every day my heart is filled with such gratitude and joy. I am truly blessed to be a Mother and my son has been instrumental in my healing journey. We are extremely close to our surrogate and she and her children remain an important part of our life and family. It was the birth of my son in 2014 followed by a cancer scare in early 2017 that really instigated my healing journey. Thankfully I got the all clear for Cancer but was diagnosed with an autoimmune disease called Coeliac Disease.

Healing is not a quick or easy journey but the rewards are breathtakingly wonderful and therefore worth every tear and every moment you feel like you can't continue, feeling it would be easier to give up and return to the life of struggle you're familiar with. You have to get to a place in your life when you've had enough of the negative cycle, the self-criticism, the fear and all that holds you back, keeps you small and suffocates your happiness and peace. Only when you are truly ready to commit to making lasting change in your internal world, will you step away from relying on quick fixes in your external world to make you happy. It is not through quick external fixes, that we find lasting happiness and peace.

These simply bring a temporary relief from the darkness we feel inside. It is only through committed, long-term internal change and hard work that we find our true self and are able to truly live in the lasting happiness we seek. So many of us live our life wishing the seconds away, waiting for the end of the day, for the weekend or our next holiday. We move house, change job, leave relationships, buy new material things and whilst it may bring about a positive change in mood initially, eventually our dark shadow, that black cloud of anxiety, sadness, fear and loneliness looms over us again. Truth is, it's always going to be there unless we address its cause and the answer to that lies within. A cliché I know but it's so true; happiness is an inside job. It took me years to finally see this and I'm so grateful for that lesson.

Just before I embarked on my healing journey, I was in the eye of my tornado. A temporary respite from its rage, a false sense of peace and stillness, covered its turbulence, which periodically shook my whole being, to remind me of its dark presence. I was at a point where I knew I had to step forward, out in to its ferocious storm and face all that swirled within it. It absolutely terrified me and I was so afraid that if I let go, I would be lost forever and consumed by its darkness. I knew that I was strong, from the very fact that I was still here and so that gave me faith and hope, that I was strong enough for the challenging road I knew was ahead of me.

And so my journey began; my path to wellness and back home to a place long forgotten, where my beautiful authentic self was patiently waiting. My healing journey has been and is still, very much about learning self-care, self-compassion, self-love, self-acceptance, forgiveness and living as my authentic self.

It's a series of stepping stones, sometimes one step forward and two back, sometimes two steps forward and one back but that in itself is a valuable lesson; to allow yourself to ebb and flow in life, just like the beautiful, powerful ocean.

My real healing journey began in April 2017, when I made the decision that enough was enough. I was fed up of the continuous cycles and tugs of war that anxiety and depression played with me and knew I had to go within, to where the real work was needed. It's just occurred to me as I write this that I actually had my first contact with my counsellor 20 years to the day of when I was diagnosed with MRKH...that, is no coincidence. For so many years I had been terrified to lose myself, to be consumed by all the emotions and trauma that I'd forced down over the years, in order to survive but here's the thing, I had already lost myself a long time ago, buried by trying to be what I thought others wanted me to be and because I had not allowed myself to feel and honour my emotions.

As hard as we try, everything we push down, eventually pushes back up and quite often this is in the form of more negative emotions like anger, bitterness and resentment and of course it often manifests as anxiety and depression. It was often in the silence of the night or moments when I was alone, that I would cry so hard that I feared my chest would split open and the pieces of my broken heart would spill out on to the floor like a split bag of rice; my mouth wide upon in agony, yet no sound escaping.

Sleep was either all consuming, swallowing up days and nights at a time, or like a dark stranger, whose visits brought haunting nightmares and night terrors. I was gripped by shame and so many negative self-beliefs of not being worthy, not being good enough and being a failure, everything's my fault, I should know this, I have to do everything on my own coupled with the fear of being rejected or abandoned. All these things have kept me small; I missed so many opportunities which prevented me from achieving so much I was capable of. When I came to realise this, I grieved the life that I had lost and was determined from that moment on that this would not continue in my life.

Though terrifying, there's something truly liberating and freeing about allowing yourself to completely fall apart and lose yourself in a tornado of emotions and feelings. That sounds crazy right and truth is, if someone had said that to me a couple of years ago, I would have looked at them like they were crazy. Society brings us up to believe that feeling our emotions and showing our feelings, is a sign of weakness and that we have to just keep going; that carrying on as if nothing's happened is what strength is. That couldn't be any further from the truth. Allowing ourselves to be vulnerable, to speak our truth, to acknowledge and respect our emotions and feelings and work with them to hear their message; that's what strength is. Emotions are what bring value to our life and the people in it. Without them we would simply be robotic and life would be mundane. They help us to understand ourselves and guide us to what's important and what's not. They are what make us real and what keeps us living instead of simply existing.

So many people simply exist in life. To live is to be vulnerable, to feel and be truly authentic. Allowing ourselves to feel our pain, means we can heal it and let it go. In that raging tornado lies the answers we seek, so we have to be brave and step forward in to it. When the dust settles, you're left feeling naked, vulnerable, fragile, broken and lost, unsure of who you are and your place in this world but in amongst the rubble where you have shed all that no longer serves you, lies the truth; your truth. It's here that you can unveil your true self and have the unique opportunity to rebuild your foundations brick by brick, in order to become the best version of yourself. So yes, revisiting all that you have buried and been hiding from is truly terrifying but with the right support, it's absolutely worth it. I dipped my toe in several times over the years but I wasn't ready and it wasn't the right time for me on those occasions. Trust your inner wisdom because it will know when the right time is and will gently guide you on to the right path to heal.

Life has taught me so much over my life to date but one thing stands out from the rest; I have a strength in me I never knew could exist and it has held me and carried me through the most turbulent of waters and ferocious storms imaginable and enabled me to battle my way through trauma, grief, loss and chronic illness to find peace and finally find my way back home, a survivor and to a life living as my authentic self. My heart and soul have always been truly at peace when I am walking through a woodland, feeling the sun on my face or am sat near the ocean listening to the waves lap on to the shore. In those moments I am at peace, my heart full of love and joy, connected to my beautiful authentic self, at one with the universe and completely in the present moment.

This is how I wanted to feel and the way I wanted to live my life; living in the present moment, aware of my emotions and all I was feeling, tasting, hearing, seeing, smelling and sensing in each and every moment. This, I thought, is what it's like to truly live rather than simply exist and this is the life I am now living.

I wrote the following poem about my authentic self and I hope it might resonate with you on some level.

I Am Your Beautiful Authentic Self

I am the truth you wish to speak, yet keep locked within, for fear of hurting another and being rejected.

I am the emotion that bubbles up but which you push back down, even though you cannot heal what you do not allow yourself to feel.

I am that feeling of peace you experience when the sun kisses your face and you hear the ocean lapping at the shore.

I am the sensations in your body you choose to ignore because you're living in the past or worrying about a future not yet come to pass.

I am that whisper of your soul you so often do not hear; drowned out by fear and negative self-talk.

I am buried under those false masks you wear, each one sculpted for a specific person.

I am suffocated by the fallacy of perfection and kept small by conformity.

I am your gut instinct that tells you when someone or something doesn't feel right.

I am that spark of light, deep within that wills you to go on, even when you're on your knees.
I am your authentic self and I hold the key to the lasting love, happiness and peace that you seek.

You've experienced a glimmer of me so many times in your life and wished for more of that peace and joy.

If only you'd surrender all that keeps you shackled, bound, gagged and living in fear.

If you could find peace with all that no longer serves you
And fall in love with yourself by embracing all of your unique imperfections, you would truly be free.

You would experience lasting inner peace and joy in their purest forms and you would be a beacon of light and an inspiration to others by being your true self; your beautiful authentic self.

My real message to you here is, let go of who you think you should be and fall in love with your everything that you are; your beautiful authentic self. When you shed your masks, let go of the negative self-talk and self-limiting beliefs and give yourself the self-compassion, love and acceptance you deserve, the life of your dreams will unfold before you, like nature blossoming in springtime.

Life is a series of ups and downs and for women, the natural cycles of our femininity also have a great impact on how we're feeling and how we handle life. The difference now for me is that I have the knowledge and skills to allow the storms of life to wash over me, instead of being totally consumed by them and the rainbow after the storm is visible a lot sooner.

I have recently been exploring Womb Healing (even though I don't have a physical womb, I still have an energetic blueprint) and charting my monthly cycle. Getting in touch with my feminine energy in this way is proving to be very enlightening and a piece of my puzzle I've been missing my whole life. The knowledge of my cycle is enabling me to work in harmony with my body, knowing when to rest and go within and when to push forward with my dreams and ideas. There's a lot of wisdom in that.

Life is a series of insights and countless opportunities for personal and spiritual growth and most are gained from the most challenging and traumatic times in our life, as our soul learns the life lessons it came here to experience. Each testing time brings with it a gift; sometimes the gift doesn't reveal itself until a much later time but there's always one there. Whilst the directions we take and the decisions we make, may not always instantly result in the outcome that we were hoping for, they often provide a link to a chain of events that leads us to where we need to be. Sometimes it's not until we reach a point in our life and look back, that we see how a series of events led us to exactly the place we needed to be, at the right time in our life. Trust in yourself and trust in the universe because it really does have your back.

I have learned to love and accept myself through acknowledging and honouring my emotions and by embracing all my perfect imperfections. I have learned to show gratitude to all the negative self-beliefs that have helped me to survive but now choose a different, more positive and self-compassionate way of thinking. I celebrate the gifts each hardship and trauma has given me because they have made me who I am today. I have learned to speak my truth, follow my intuition, stay in the present moment and stay in tune with my body sensations and by doing so I have found my authentic self and am experiencing lasting inner peace and joy in their purest form.

The whispers of my soul have spoken to me my whole life about love, hope and belief and showed me that there is too much beauty in the world to give up, despite all the pain and suffering we experience. My inner light has guided me home to my authentic self. A place of peace, where self-love and self-acceptance live harmoniously and true happiness and joy are permanent residents. To give you an idea of what it felt like for me when everything I had been working on so hard, came together in one beautiful epiphany, shining a light on my beautiful authentic self, I wrote the following poem after I got home on the final day of attending a three-day Equine Facilitated Learning workshop, called Connect with your Authentic Self.

FINALLY, I AM HOME

As I emerged back out into normal life
The world seemed different somehow.
It was almost as if I had been reborn
And was seeing the world with new, curious eyes.

There was a stillness I have never experienced,
A quiet and gentle knowing
And a sense of belonging.
The many masks I have worn as my false self, had been removed.

The sunlight seemed brighter,
The cool air, clean and fresh, tingled on my face,
My senses heightened with a new awareness.
What was it that's changed, I thought.

The world I witnessed was just as it was the day I started,
Yet something was different.
The change I was feeling was from a place deep within,
A place that had been long forgotten.

Buried, kept small and hidden.
Shackled by the fear of shame
And bound by conformity,
Starved of all it ever longed for.

A new-found sense of freedom sent waves of joy through my body
And hot, cleansing tears of relief trickled down my face.
A feeling of immense gratitude filled my heart,
As I tried to make sense of the most profound and insightful
experience of my life.

Yet I was unable to find the words to describe something so
magical. Finally, I am home.
Back in the saddle of trust, The reins of control released.
I choose to run in the wind of belief,
Secure in the knowledge that everything I need is within me.

Everyone's healing journey is unique but ultimately starts with the acknowledgement that something needs to change. There is no one-size fits all and it's trial and error to find exactly what feels right for you. The key thing to remember is to follow your intuition, follow where your heart guides you and your soul will tell you what feels right through feelings of comfort, peace, joy, euphoria, insights and enlightenment.

It is vital to have support from people who make you feel, safe, held, nurtured and not judged in any way. At the beginning of 2017 I found those people for myself, when a close friend told me about a spiritual group of like-minded souls that she belonged to on Facebook and so I joined 'Discover Your Purpose'.

I had always been highly sensitive to my environment and the people around me. I instinctively knew things that I had no way of knowing, knew what people were feeling because I literally felt it and had several experiences with spirits, having seen, heard and sensed many things over the years. Finally, I was surrounded by people just like me.
The group were and are incredibly supportive and everything I needed to support my healing, which led me on a journey of spiritual awakening.

I've met some very significant people in my life, who have been and still are, instrumental in my healing journey. It was where I met my Holistic Counsellor, a truly wonderful and very gifted lady, who has held my hand during my journey and with whom I have talked about things that I have never talked about with anyone else and cried tears that I have usually kept for private. She has provided me with a safe and nurturing space to explore all the pain, the sadness and repressed emotions and feelings that have been locked away deep inside of me for years. She has believed in me, seen and heard me and understood me in ways I have never experienced and this has given me the most nourishing environment in which to grow.

Throughout my healing journey I have had many revelations about my wounded inner child, how my past often plays out in my present, worked on recognising and changing my negative self-beliefs and patterns of self-sabotage, understanding my relationship with my Parents, revisiting my wounds and looking at how the traumatic things I have experienced have affected me and caused the shame and fear in my life.

I have looked at myself in a truly holistic manner and been addressing imbalances in my body, mind, soul and energetic self, in the following ways:

* **Physical** – Nutrition, Vitamins, Exercise and Rest and Relaxation.
* **Mind** – Counselling, Meditation, Mindfulness, Creative and Written Journaling, Reading self-help/personal development books, Focusing on and learning self-care and self-compassion, Vision Boards, Coaching/Mentoring, Aromatherapy oils, Hypnotherapy, Affirmations and Setting Intentions.
* **Soul** – Tarot/Oracle cards, Shamanic Soul Retrieval, Listening and moving to music and Spending time in nature.
* **Energetic Self** – Restoring balance through Reiki, Crystals, exploring and learning more about the Chakra system.

I have also been working on recognising and setting boundaries, speaking my truth and expressing my needs, looking at ancestral links, recognising my triggers, exploring my shadow side (the side of us where the more negative emotions live such as anger and jealousy), acknowledging, honouring, expressing and recognising my emotions (good and bad) and using body scanning and their associated body sensations and emotions, as information to help me better understand myself, communicate my needs and speak with love.

I am eternally grateful that I reached a point in my life where I thought enough is enough, I no longer wanted to continue to live in a cycle of pain; I didn't want to grow old with such pain in my heart, for it to turn in to anger, bitterness and resentment. I wanted to be happy, to truly create a happy and fulfilled life, where I found myself and learned to love all that I am. We frequently look to an external source to fix us, desperately seeking an answer and an end to our pain but ultimately the responsibility and the power lies within us. We are the only person that can change us, heal ourselves and put pain to rest, to make way for a brighter and happier future.

Of course we often need the support of others, whilst doing this but unless you're fully invested in putting the work in for yourself, then the best healer, mentor, coach or counsellor in the world cannot help you. We have to be ready to face our demons head on and commit to making positive change and keep going, even when the going gets tough.

Today, I am more balanced, happier, calmer, more at peace and most importantly I recognise my own self-worth and I am finally giving myself the self-compassion, acceptance and love that I've needed my whole life.

It takes great patience and courage to embark on and stay committed to a healing journey but it is so worth it. No matter how small the progress made may seem, remember every small step adds up and results in the most miraculous gift. There is nothing more beautiful than a soul blossoming into life, as its authentic self.

Here're my top tips on taking those first steps:

* **Self-compassion** – Treat yourself with the same love, patience and kindness that you'd treat someone close to you, like your best friend. So when you make a mistake or something doesn't go to plan, rather than give yourself a hard time, think about what you'd say to your best friend if they came to you for advice or support. Self-compassion is vital to your happiness and inner peace.

* **Self-care** – Do something every day, as a gesture of love and kindness to yourself. It doesn't have to be anything big or extravagant, it can simply be factoring time in to your day just for you, to take a candlelit bubble bath, snuggle up to read a book, watch your favourite film or TV programme, go for a walk out in nature, play your favourite music, get creative through painting or creative journaling, or any way you feel drawn to. Anything that makes you feel good.

* **Gratitude** – start a Gratitude Jar or Journal where you can record all the things you're grateful for on a daily basis. Don't just think about the big things, it's the little things like, hearing your favourite song on the radio, something that made you smile or laugh, something beautiful in nature you noticed, a compliment someone gave you, being grateful for your home, your car, your health, your job, your family, etc.

* **Support** – Having someone you can go to, who you know will listen with empathy and provide you with a safe, positive, nurturing, non-judgmental and compassionate space for you will really help. You might want to consider seeking the support of a counsellor, mentor or coach and/or join a group of like-minded people.

* **Create a Thumbs Down List** – Start thinking about your boundaries and what needs to change in order to make life simpler, easier and more peaceful. Examples include: "I no longer let anyone speak rudely to me". "I no longer say yes to things that don't make me happy." "I will no longer rush through my day."

I hope that my story inspires you and gives you hope to keep stepping forward in your journey, safe in the knowledge that everything you need is within you to heal and live the life your heart and soul are gently guiding you to. Finally, I'd like to leave you with this blessing from my heart and The House of Harmony's heart to yours.

Harmony Blessing

May the light of your soul always guide you home.
May love fill your heart, so you never feel alone.
May hope keep you strong, even when you're on your knees.
May your being be nourished by the animals, oceans and trees.
And so it is.

-End-

THE GIRL IN THE DARK
By
Lex Envy

I see her
A girl. Small and fragile. In the darkness
I call to her
She does not hear me.

I walk closer. Quietly. Carefully.
This...is a dark place. Full of shadows, demons and nightmares
They know I am here.
They know she is here and they are coming for us.

Why is she here? Who is she?
I have been in this dark a long time.
She is just a child. How did she even get here?
I am near her. She is aware I am close.

She puts out a trusting hand to me.
"Help me" she says
I see her face.
It is familiar. I have seen her before.

I take her tiny hand and suddenly... I remember.
I remember that day. I remember the pain and the despair.
I remember how lost I felt. How utterly alone I was.

"You left me here" she says with tears in her eyes
"That day. You left me behind. You forgot about me. You left me here
in the dark. To fight. To struggle. Alone."

"How could I? I don't even know you?" I say defensively.
"You know me better than anyone. I have been here much longer
than you" she cries.

I look at her. The girl in the dark. Standing in front of me. Tiny.
Innocent. Longing for love and care.

She...is me. I...am her.

I did leave her. I broke away and forgot her. I left her behind in the darkness.
How could I have been so cruel?

I embrace her like my own child. I tell her that I am sorry and that I love her with my whole heart. That everything is ok now.

I have come back for her. I WILL free her from this darkness.
I will fight the demons that are coming for us.
And she WILL see the light again.

www.lexenvy.com

-End-

THE NIGHT I FELT I LOST EVERYTHING!
By
Victoria Baker

Friday February 27th 1998 I was just 6 years of age at this time, I do not really remember much of the day time on this particular day. I have tried to write as much as I can remember, other parts are added by what my Dad and Brother recall of that day and have told me.

On this Friday I was downstairs with my Dad and older Brother, my Mom was fast asleep upstairs, or so we believed. My Mom used to go to bed during the day as she worked night shifts. I remember she always used to set an alarm for around 8pm or 9pm to get up and get ready for work.

So myself and my Brother was able to stay up late due to it been a Friday, so myself and my Brother and Dad were watching TV in the living room and I remember hearing my Mom's alarm clock start to go off which was normal. After a few moments I realised it was still going off, I then said to my Dad that Mom's alarm is still going off. We all just thought maybe she was already up before her alarm and getting ready in the bathroom and she couldn't turn it off at the time. We continued to watch TV but found it strange that the alarm got very loud and continued for longer than normal.

My Dad asked me and my Brother to go wake up Mom or check where she was and turn the alarm off. Me and my Brother raced up the stairs laughing and joking we both wanted to be the first person to get to Mom. It was a very funny moment. We ran into Mom and Dad's room and our Mom was on top of the bed with her arms wide open. We both thought nothing of this and I remember trying to talk to my Mom. My Brother was quiet and white as a ghost, whereas I didn't see anything wrong. I was all happy trying to talk to my Mom.

My Brother told me to get off the bed and move away from Mom and he ran screaming for my Dad. I remember that when my Brother told me to get off the bed, I began feeling confused and I just wanted to hug her. While my Brother was getting my Dad I stood very quietly by the window with my fingers in my mouth, biting my nails, which I had never done before. Standing there I didn't cry even though I felt I knew what was going on, my Dad and Brother came upstairs. I do not remember too much about that, but I do remember My Dad telling my Brother and I to go downstairs, so I held my Brother's hand and we walked away,

When I looked back before we walked down the stairs I saw my Dad trying to help her, but I knew she was gone. We walked downstairs and the whole house felt weird; not normal. I sat on the sofa and waited. I didn't say much, I looked at the door in the hope that she would walk into the living room as usual. My Dad called an ambulance and then told my Brother to call my Nan. Time passed by then we heard a movement upstairs. All of a sudden, my Dad came rushing down the stairs from top to bottom, he couldn't stand properly he was saying to my Brother "She has gone Martin! Your Mom has gone!"

Not long after, I remember the ambulance arriving followed by my Nan and her partner. The ambulance team were upstairs for a while with my Dad, and then the policeman and woman arrived. I do not remember much of this part it is a blur to me. They took my Mom from our home in the ambulance. When she was gone I had to go upstairs and pack a few clothes in a bag to stay away at my Nan's. I remember looking at where I had last saw my Mom. I was in complete shock, staring into the bedroom. I saw that my Dad had been sick all over the floor, I felt like I was in a dream and this was not real. My Nan then pushed me along to go get my stuff together quickly. I felt I had no life and the happy little girl I was beforehand had gone, the past hour had taken its toll. My Dad and Nan went with the police behind the ambulance and my Brother and I went to my Nan's house with her partner.

Next, I remember being at my Nan's house, where me my Brother and Nan's partner were all in the living room with blankets over us. Nan's partner went straight to sleep while my Brother took a while but eventually fell off to sleep for a bit, I on the other hand did not go to sleep. I sat and stared at the frosted glass door, hoping and praying; I just didn't believe it was real. I then started to see someone behind the glass. I got scared and put my head under the blanket. I remember thinking "Who is that? That's not someone who should be here with us". We were the only three in the house. I slowly looked again but there was no one there. Then the lamps went off and back on again. This scared me even more and I retreated back under the blanket once more; I just didn't want to look. I tried to pull my head from the covers but fear had gripped me. I tried to force myself to sleep but couldn't as I was very afraid and felt very alone. I eventually got the courage to uncover myself and looked around once more.

Someone was at the door again; I didn't know what to do other than to try to wake my Nan's partner. I slowly walked toward him, whilst staring at the door and at the figure staring back. It started walking left to right passing the door. I was so panicked I woke Nan's partner. I told him someone was behind the door; he shot up thinking it was my Nan and Dad, and went to look.

I remember following him to the door with my blanket over me, Nan's partner could see no one around and headed to the kitchen. I stood at the living room door looking down the hallway, as he looked around the hall and kitchen. Opposite me was the staircase; I looked up and saw someone's legs at the very top moving left to right again. I was terrified and couldn't call to my Nan's partner. I looked behind me and my Brother was still asleep; I felt I had lost my voice. My Nan's partner then came walking towards me and I pointed to the top of the stairs. He went up and looked around. He come back down and whispered: "No one is there Vicky". He made his way back in to the living room with me following him, and told me to get some sleep. He sat back in his chair and fell right back to sleep instantly.

Time passed and I started to hear talking coming from the hall, I was so scared I just wanted someone to wake up and be with me. After what felt like forever my Dad and Nan arrived back with the police. I remember being told by the policewoman that Mom had died at home. I cannot remember crying a lot at all I must have blocked it all out. I just felt lost and alone, the rest of this night has faded from my memory.

So that was the night I will never forget, I know there was more but I believe I have blocked this out. Each day growing up got harder and harder. We have been through many struggles, I felt so empty and had no interest in anyone; not truly. And still to this day I struggle in social group situations.

I missed her so much when I hit my first birthday without her. There were no Mommy hugs nor kisses in bed, no seeing her when downstairs with music and balloons, no watching me open my gifts from her. I missed her curling my hair ready for the day ahead, I just missed every little thing about her. You name it I missed it all.

Christmas was not Christmas anymore I hated it. Christmas was my Mom's favourite time of the year. I'd never felt so lost in my life; I didn't feel like a child any more it had all been snatched away from me.

I spent a while living with my other Nan and Grandad Baker and have some fond memories of this time. When I went back to school I was bullied straight away. Just because my Mom had died, they thought it was ok to bully me for it. This hurt me; pained me mentally. I just didn't trust anyone anymore. I also missed a lot of school with the whole situation and this in turn, made me fall behind other students and get bad grades. It was one thing after another; this is what made me lose trust in people. I pushed them away. It didn't matter if they were trying to help or not. They were all the same to me.

So lots of things happened whilst growing up, stuff that has mentally scarred me and upon which I could speak forever. I am now 26 and not one day passes that I do not miss Mom. We will never forget our loved ones, but the pain gets that little bit easier to cope with, as time goes by. My family helped me get through it.

I met a man in my college years; the love of my life, my rock, my soulmate. We have been together for over nine years. I trust him and he understands me deeply. He knows what to say and do to make me happy. I have noticed too that my creative talents, spiritual gifts and dreams became stronger the more I grew as a person.

The spiritual gifts and talents were passed down from my Mom, but unfortunately we didn't find out about a certain dream, that plagued my Mom for months before her death, until afterward.

Her best friend approached my Dad and explained to him that Mom had been having dreams about being taken away in an ambulance with her deceased Father, my Grandad, sat beside her as she was taken away. We felt by hearing this story that Mom was not alone when she passed and that comforted us a little.

My one true passion and the thing that I did most from the age of seven was my art. I loved drawing it gave me comfort, and pulled me away from the dark places in my mind. I could not let myself be pulled in. I had to prove to Mom and myself that I could achieve; the darkness would never win, not in this lifetime! So when I left school I went to college and did art and design courses one after another for 4 years. I became a student of distinction and even have awards sitting on my shelf. I am confident that my Mom will be proud of me and this makes me proud of myself. So I can say that art has been a good thing for me, helping express loss and love.

From the bottom of my heart I can honestly say creativity in your life can help you too, not just art but music, pottery, acting, the list goes on. When I was little I also used to love watching Disney films curled up on the sofa. This can work wonders on a down-day, but my art made me feel like I was in Neverland; a place where no one could hurt me.

I want to say to anyone who has experienced loss, that everything is OK and will be OK. You might not see it at the moment, but you will all find the light. Once again, the key is to allow yourself to carry on living life to the fullest, like those lost would want you to. They'll be proud whatever you do. I know it's extremely hard, but remember it's OK to miss someone, we must also remember not to let the darkness beat us, we are creatures of light and love, and love conquers all.

I wish you all the best in your future, and will leave you with a quote my partner loves:

"The future is a mystery,
the past is history,
and the now is a gift,
that's why it's called the present."

(If I can do it, you can do it!)

In loving memory of Kathleen Ann Baker,
a loving Mother, Wife, Sister and Daughter.
(03/09/1961 - 27/02/1998)

-End-

OH HOW IT FEELS.
By
Andrew Rowles

Oh how it feels good
When I was having fun,
Oh how it felt good
When I was being the rebel.
Oh how it feels good
When the drink became my friend
Oh how it feels bad
When the drink made me ill.

Oh how it feels bad
When you run with the wrong crowd,
Oh how it feels bad
When your friends turn on you.
Oh how it feels bad
When steel cut my skin,
Oh how it feels bad
When I looked at my scars.

Oh how it feels bad
When you think you have reached your lowest.
Oh how it feels,
Oh how it feels.

Oh how it feels good,
when I got a new job.

Oh how it feels good
When lady light entered my life,
Oh how it feels good
When she showed me love,
Oh how it feels good
when we fought for each other.

Oh how it feels good
When we moved in together,
Oh how it feels good
When we moved to the country.

Oh how it feels,
Oh how it feels
Oh how I feel;
GREAT

We live once; never look back, look forward to the future.
Live in the moment.

Andrew Rowles
The love of Victoria Baker's life

LIGHTWORKERS UNITED
By
S.A.M.

We are all but visitors
upon this earthly plane
We strive to make our lives complete
Until we go home once again
~~~

Some things are sent to try us
Obstacles hurdles too
Sometimes we have to wipe them out
Sometimes we must go through.
~~~

Sometimes we need to ask for help
It may go against the grain
Yet help is all around us
until; we go home once again.
~~~

Look how things are changing
Is the message getting through?
People seem to notice more
It reflects in things they do.
~~~

Messengers are not frowned upon
The way they used to be
People seeking spiritual help
Can be open, can be free.
~~~

Why is this? I ask myself
What is it that has changed?
Thoughts and prayers are still the same
Though, beliefs are rearranged.
~~~

Don't rest on your laurels
Keep on pushing you'll be heard
Our Angels will stand by us all
Love will spread the word.

*"Sometimes we are forced to go through difficult situations, because we
need the experience to be able to identify
our soul purpose."*

Cath B

WHEN YOU'RE TOLD
"YOU'RE NOT GOOD ENOUGH"
By
Carolyn Louise Pearse

The dread of going to work, the anxiety I felt, the strange feeling of not being where I should be whilst on my journey to work; I felt like I didn't belong. I was lost.

When I was in school I always dreamt about working in design and fashion, doing something creative. One day whilst I was in an A-level textile class my teacher made a comment and whether she meant it or not, it would change my whole life. She said, "You're not good enough". From that moment on, the path of my life changed. I no longer felt that I could follow my dreams of going to University to study fashion. It shattered my confidence and I pretty much gave up.

I went on to do a degree in Event Management. Don't get me wrong I enjoyed my degree, I had completed an Enterprise project as part of my dissertation in my final year where I wrote a business plan and more or less set up a business (without actually setting it up). My tutor told me it was a viable business idea and I could really make it work, but my confidence was low and I didn't really believe I could make it work. I was young and I had no experience – how could I possibly run my own business?! But I'd caught the entrepreneurship bug and I knew one day I wanted to have my own business. So I graduated and went down the traditional path, conformed to society and got a job. A job that was in no way related to my degree, in no way related to my childhood passion of fashion and design, but it was a job, it was secure, it paid the bills and it was what I was 'supposed' to do. I hated it.

Fast forward a couple of years and I ended up going down a career path of Marketing & PR. I enjoyed it and did well in my career but it didn't fulfil me, I got bored easily and moved around from job to job trying to find that one role that would light me up and relight the fire in my belly again.

10 years went by, it had just turned 2016 – the year I was turning 30. As I sat on the bus to work in the morning I felt a sense of sadness that I wasn't doing something I loved. Had I wasted the last 10 years of my life? If I didn't take action now, I felt sick with the thought that in another 10 years I would still be in exactly the same position. The only person who could change my life, was me. Enough was enough. Enough of worrying what other people think. Enough of not feeling good enough.

In 2016 I started my entrepreneurial journey. I hired a coach who helped me put the things I needed in place to start a business, to develop my mindset and face my fears. Don't get me wrong it hasn't been an easy journey but I've loved it and I have developed and learnt so much over the past year.

It's funny the path that life takes you sometimes. I have now joined together my love of branding from my marketing career and my passion of design and style to create my business as a brand consultant and stylist. Helping creative entrepreneurs style their brand that is truly aligned with their core values, personality, passion and personal style, creating a business that they love and a brand that sparkles, makes me sparkle too.

Looking back I don't regret the choices I made. I don't even blame my teacher about what she said. In fact I am grateful, because without that comment maybe I wouldn't have as much determination or passion as I do now and I possibly wouldn't be where I am today.

My mission is to ensure that no-one ever feels as stuck, lonely or as overwhelmed as I did. If someone has a passion and a dream then they have every right to follow that dream. Your dreams belong to you for a reason. Everyone deserves to sparkle and to do that we need to do what we love, follow our passion and be true to ourselves.

-End-

MY JOURNEY; PERFECTLY IMPERFECT
By
Donna-Michelle

Well they say that life is a journey and not a destination, and I think that seems pretty correct. I often envy people who do not worry, or do not really feel much empathy; their life I think must be pretty straightforward and logical. I on the other hand, am an empath. I am sensitive; some would say over-sensitive and they would be right.

My life has always been fraught as I struggle to make sense of my character, my desire to be needed, and loved, my ability to talk myself out of so much through low self-esteem, which later would be validated by others as I made poor choices with whom I allowed into my life.

I have always been a caring sort, always wanting to find a fix for anyone in pain or suffering, I worry about people endlessly and a glance at a negative newsfeed or media piece can play on my mind for days. I have even watched people struggle on TV and literally tracked them down to offer my help, I still proudly own a letter received as a teenager in response to my letter I sent to a teenage boy who was suffering cancer and who had featured in a National Newspaper. I needed these people to know I was thinking of them. There have been many other examples. I have tried to rescue many people. The trouble is, who needed rescuing at times, was in fact, me and this is my constant lesson.

I have often focused more on fixing others than in fact allowing myself to focus on me. Not in an indulgent pretentious way, but in a gentle, encouraging way to myself, for myself. I think many of us are guilty of that aren't we? We digress, procrastinate, we get absorbed in quick fixes of distraction, social media, drama, all the chores and expectations we limit ourselves with. All the escaping from that which we really need to focus on, being healthy in body and in mind.

I reflect a lot, I do not think that is a bad thing; I do not regret much, although of course I wish I had made less hasty decisions, and been less of a people pleaser at times. I wish I had been more assertive and had more self-belief, but I feel I am constantly learning, and as I reflect, I realise my inner strength is way more than I give myself credit for.

It was always laughed about that I was the black sheep of my family. I was always a nice person, I always cared and was there for everyone, but I was the spirited one. I made the stupid life decisions, I did not go in for the dating, engagement, marriage and children thing. I was hasty, desperate to feel loved and be loved, and I had my heart on my sleeve repeatedly. I wanted all that and more but never went about it the right way, there was no substance, no maturity, to my relationships. I realise as I age, that the person I need to feel love from most of all is myself. I am still learning this.

Life can be hurtful. Scrap that. People can be hurtful. People can make you feel devalued and beneath them. Of course, we choose whether to allow that or not. I have spent a long part of my life feeling inferior to others, I am not really sure why. We could study nature, nurture and life experience, but I know, at the age of 41 I have grown so much as a person, and that the journey I am making sees me growing further still.

I am learning through circumstance, that I cannot fix everything. My goodness, that has brought up feelings of failure, hopelessness, resentment, frustration, and sadness. Overwhelming sadness.

Both of my girls have chronic health conditions and I am now a Carer. This is my identity for now. How I view that is work in progress. It can make me feel overwhelmed with responsibility, with a need to just make everything ok, but I know that I cannot be that person who puts a sticking plaster on this, I cannot find a solution, a resolve, and that has been hard.

I am learning that it is okay to be honest about those feelings, that some things I cannot mend, but my purpose here is to fill my girls' hearts with love and purpose, and to show them they can and will achieve anything.

I hope to help them realise their dreams a little more readily and more confidently than I did, and for them to know that they can make a difference in the world, but can do so whilst holding their own, protecting themselves, and demanding a certain level of respect along the way.

Circumstances are different to what I had anticipated for this time in my life. Due to health issues we have much less freedom and some days are overwhelming and feel relentless. The bottom line is we are able to find joy in little things. We can plan big days out and have those moments to look forward to and just create memories with what we have right here and now. I need to stop sweating the small stuff, stop giving all of myself to others and start loving myself and give myself credit for all that I do achieve.

I am a Carer. I am a mother. I am an advocate for M.E and Type 1 Diabetes, I am a fundraiser, I run two Charity Groups, I am doing a Degree in Psychology, I am...........

Those two words are so powerful aren't they?... "I am." What we say inwardly to ourselves, or what we convey to others, is so deep-seated, so powerful, it will either feed you negativity or positivity. I am enough. I am worthy. I am stronger than I think. I am not able to fix this, but I can make things easier or at least more tolerable......

I am Donna. I am a mother, and a Carer, and the important thing is that every day I show up to be the best person I can be, to be patient loving and kind.

Some days that may mean me with unkempt hair and my slouchies, some days, hell!

My house could be compared to the Waltons', all clean and organised, with ten vegetable variations thrown into that wholesome tea. I can never really tell to be honest, and that is ok. I am learning, that it is ok not to be ok, it is alright to admit that. I can and should allow others to support me, as well as me being the supporter.

This journey I am on sometimes it feels like I am lunging and lurching through it, and then other days I feel like the weight has lifted, and that things are just easier, not perfect, but that things are ok. Perfectly imperfect I guess, but we are right here where we are meant to be. The love and team effort behind the girls and I is a force to be reckoned with regardless. We see humour in stupid stuff, and we are a great support to each other.

As a person, I am learning that self-love is not indulgent, it is a necessity; some days I am better at it than others. I will stock up in Holland and Barrett and take various things to support my body, I will lie in magnesium bath salts and do some yoga and meditation... my goal is to keep these things as a regular integral part of my daily life, and to support myself instead of waiting for those lunging sadder days.

We are each a work in progress, some of us have not realised that yet or are not sufficiently self-aware. Others have been too self-aware for too long.

I look forward to my life's journey being about more balance, more harmony, more self-love and a greater sense of what I can achieve, instead of all the things I cannot. I wish this for you too.

With love and blessings,
Donna-Michelle

-End-

HELLO BEAUTIFUL
By
Beth James

Hello beautiful! I know you can't hear me. I know you can't see me. And, hey, you wouldn't listen to me if you could! But I hear you. I see you. I feel your fear. I remember your terror. The incomprehension in your eyes. The shock, swiftly followed by a silent rage. The sleepless nights spent waiting. Waiting for something to happen. Waiting for something not to happen. A childhood wasted waiting. Waiting for the inevitable. Waiting for pain. Waiting for hurt. Waiting for the silent tears to flow. Waiting for someone to look into your eyes and see the agony. But no one ever looked. Waiting for someone to hear the story you could never speak. But no one ever heard.

Then, innocence lost, you were brave my love. You got up and left. Your imprisoner had left the door unlocked, little expecting you to just up and go. You stepped out into the void unknowing, uncaring, and unseeing.

No matter how impoverished, we all have a gift. Yours was, and still is, courage my love. That huge lion heart of yours has both served you well and cost you dearly.

What courage! What faith! What trust! You had it all in buckets and simply looked up at the sky with that inner knowing. Knowing that despite everything, life would be magical. Knowing that somehow you would be looked after. Knowing that one fine day you would wake up happy.

Truly deeply madly happy.
Even so, you wouldn't have believed me then if I'd appeared to you that day and showed myself to you as I am now. It would have been incomprehensible to you how you could have become so confident. So self-assured. So content and fulfilled.

How you could have two beautiful grown sons who still wrap their arms around you and laughing, tell you how much they love you.

You'd not have believed the room I sit in now writing this – full of memories from your travels; treasures from those who have loved you; gifts from friends newly made.

You certainly couldn't have comprehended how I now earn my living from your life's passion – my work is my life and my life is my work.

You wouldn't be surprised though at just how much your understanding of and connection to the moon grew over the years. How much time you have spent gazing at her and how your hair once red has grown white – though may be purple next week!

Your precious life is now spent loving and doing and growing. No more waiting. For you sleep comes easy now. You awaken with excitement and gratitude for each dawning day. You laugh a lot. Sometimes you cry, but never for long. You are proud. Proud of the life you've lived, of the scars you bear. Of the road you've travelled.

But most of all, my love, I am proud of you. For stepping out and stepping up. For taking life by the horns and saying, "Hey I want to play!" For having the courage and determination to keep at it. To keep on playing the transformation game year in year out. For never, ever giving up. Because of you, I am now me. And life has never been better.

Whoever you are, wherever you are, whatever deep, dark, dreadful place it is you find yourself in, that holds you back in fear, in desperation, isolated and confused – please, please, please know that there is a far greater purpose to all things.

Know that you are loved, that you are held, and that one fine day you truly can be all those things you dream of and more.

-End-

JOURNEY OF THE WHITEBEAR
By
Evelyn Whitebear

I spent most of my childhood days outdoors, as we did back in those days!

I remember my early childhood at school where I felt tiny and was easily picked on. How did such young children get so mean? So much jealousy. It was hard to deal with. Whenever I made anything, another child would somehow ruin it. I couldn't understand this behaviour. I used to draw a lot of patterns with bright colours, but the teacher told me I had to draw other things and forbade me from drawing any more. It seemed that from a young age I wouldn't be allowed to be myself, and would be stifled and controlled.

When I was six my parents moved us to Wales, but I wondered how we were going to live in a Whale, it sounded a bit cramped! But where we moved to was a picturesque village in the well of a valley, surrounded by nature. A stream flowed past the cottage and through our little orchard, and off into the distance. I would play for hours in the stream, watching the water boatmen skimming across the surface of the water, and tiny tiddlers swimming underneath. It was here that I connected wholeheartedly with nature and its perfectly peaceful natural flow of life. I picked flowers, sometimes fruit, made dens and climbed trees. When I wasn't outside I would draw and paint. Mostly trees and birds, I loved drawing birds.

Inside the house we had resident ghosts. We didn't see them often but we had some strange experiences. Yes, it frightened me, but it didn't bother me on a daily basis. The door of my room would sometimes flick off its catch and open slightly, but we got used to it.

One night I woke from a nightmare and called out for my Mum. A shadowy figure rushed into the room and came over to the bed. I thought it was my Mother. I threw my arms around her but, nothing was there! My arms grabbed on to nothingness! My heart almost stopped! I shrank down under the covers and hid, and eventually fell asleep. That was the last time I called out for my Mother.

Now and again my Dad would wake in the night to see a woman standing over the bed looking at him. Guests who stayed would see the same thing. I started to become quite sensitive to spirits and began to feel and see them in other 'haunted' places. I loved this place, it really felt like home in so many ways.

When I was 11 we sadly had to move away from my paradise and back into the 'real world'. But to me it was alien, too many houses, too many people, and I knew I'd never fit in. I left part of my soul back in the Welsh Valley, sitting in the tree, a part of nature, always. In my new world I immersed myself in music, listening to the top 20 and the occasional album that belonged to my Mother or my Sister, as I wasn't allowed to buy my own until I reached my teens. I also learned to play my own music. I already played piano but now learned to play the flute, violin and guitar. Just a little. My poems of nature became poems of life as nature became distant and I made friends with concrete and brick.

At 13 I was totally lost. I wanted to become a Nun. I withdrew from the word. I became ill. It started off as Tonsillitis, and the doctor filled me with Penicillin. I started getting worse so higher doses of Penicillin. My throat swelled so much I couldn't eat and could barely drink. The doctor said I had glandular fever and upped the Penicillin doses even further. It didn't work. I now weighed 6 stone and became so weak I couldn't even sit up in bed. My Mother fed me jelly, but even that was too painful to eat. I was skeletal. I do not know why I hadn't been admitted to the hospital for tests. I felt rejected, left alone all day while my Parents went to work. None of my friends ever came to visit. I felt that I was on my death bed. I just lay there, falling in and out of sleep. After about four weeks of this quackery, the doctor decided to try a different antibiotic and miraculously the swellings in my throat soon started to subside. The Doctor at last came to the conclusion that I was allergic to Penicillin. If he hadn't changed my medication when he did I would have died.

A month later I could walk again, if I held onto something. It took a further month for me to get fully well again. I was sad that none of my friends had visited while I was ill, and rarely called on the phone. I had been forgotten and I felt dislocated from normal life, which had moved on without me. Back at school I was so behind with everything I had no way of catching up. I ditched the complicated science subjects that I had been so good at, and focused on art and English. I found new friends.

But things were to change again. When I was 14 my Mother decided to introduce me to Transcendental Meditation and I began to meditate regularly. I loved the initiation ceremony, it really opened up my eyes to another world. At first I found meditating in this way a little too much and I released so much frustration and stress far too quickly, so I would break down in tears for no reason, fairly often. My practising time was cut down and eventually I levelled out again. When I meditated I would see purple and orange pulsating light, with an eye in the centre. I was told that not everyone saw this during meditation and it was rare and special.

A few months later we moved again, further into the town where there were even fewer trees. My Parents had separated and it hit me hard. I was close to my Dad and I rarely saw him again, becoming distant to my Mother who was controlling, narcissistic, and stressed! It wasn't a good time for any of us, so I immersed myself even deeper into music and art, and meditation. My Mother had a new boyfriend, my Sister had moved in with her new Husband, and I felt more alone than ever before. I left home at 16, a couple of months before I turned 17. Two years later I moved to London.

A lot happened over the next few years and by the time I was 26 I had been married, divorced and become Mother to two children. I read a lot, and turned my attention to books and tarot cards. I read about life after death, out-of-body experiences, and Witchcraft. Witchcraft fascinated me as I loved the connection with the natural world. I later found out that my Great Grandmother used to read tea leaves, and my Father was psychic. I myself had many premonitions in dreams, though nothing too dramatic. I then started reading about aliens, and abductions. I noticed I was having some strange experiences, like losing time when travelling, finding biopsy holes in my leg, and having dreams where bright lights were shining down on me and people where moving around me. I woke up in a panic screaming, "You're not my dentist, you're not my dentist!" The next morning I found a hole in my tooth under my crown which I wasn't happy about! Was it a coincidence that strange things were happening? Were things happening because I was reading the books? Or had I been guided to reading the books to help me understand what was happening?

My daughter had a strange dream when she was about 5. She didn't know about any of the books I was reading. She told me that she woke in the night and there were 'Stealers' in her room. Stealers were little blue men who took people away. They took her and her Brother out of their room and they floated up to a place in the sky, but a lovely tall lady in a white flowing gown told the Stealers not to take them, and she brought them both back to their room, safe and sound.

Backtracking slightly, my marriage had been quite a horrendous experience. My Husband was a narcissistic schizophrenic psychopath. Yes, I know how to find them! He was the master of disguise as so many narcissists are, and I'd come to know a kind and gentle side of him. The Hyde side of his character soon emerged though, once I was trapped in the relationship. He made sure all my friends disappeared by telling them nasty stories about me behind my back. My family more or less disowned me because they didn't like him. They didn't help me, they said it was my decision to be with him, and left me to my fate. Most of the time he was fine and we got on well, like two peas in a pod, but every few months he would have a few days of scary behaviour. I had no one else to turn to, but him.

Narcissists are really clever. They will make sure that you have no one else to run to. They will hurt you emotionally, mentally and sometimes physically, to the point where you are beside yourself, frightened and in despair. And then they come straight in with love and care, they put their arms around you and promise they'll never be like that again because they love you so much. You need a hug, you need safety, and you respond to the hugs and false words. What else can you do? He eventually manipulated me into starting a family, but soon after the children came he became more and more stressed and things became really bad. The threats to my life started and I started to fear for the children. One day he made me pack my bags and threw me out, without the children. A Mother's nightmare! Eventually I managed to persuade him that things were good and the children needed me, and that he wouldn't cope on his own. He let me back. But a week later I left early in the morning while he was asleep, with the children. Life wasn't easy for a long time after that. I would lie awake in bed thinking he would find me and kill me. He had promised me I'd be looking over my shoulder for the rest of my life. I almost went off the rails, but thankfully the children kept me focused. Gradually I remembered to meditate and I started my healing journey.

The scars from this 5-year episode of my life were deep. I decided to learn hypnotherapy, and surrounded myself with crystals. The healing was slow. A new man came into my life who helped me through the difficult, low moments, at least for a short while. I married a second time, and everything was rosy. We bought a house and for a few years had a lovely life. Things were calm and I could continued to focus on my spiritual path and my healing. My book reading continued and I was guided to read a book called The Only Planet of Choice. It really changed my life. It was a book of channelled information from the 60's and 70's, about the originals of the different races on Earth. One day one of my clients saw the book and told me she went to a channelling group and I should come along, which I did.

At first I found channelling quite difficult to do. The lovely lady that ran the group suggested I learn Reiki as it would help to open up my channels. So I did, and it did, and I soon learned how to channel. The messages were amazing and the energy was beautiful, and I soon became fully addicted to it. To this day it is still my favourite occupation. Having learned Reiki, I now practised self-healing. Whenever I felt anxiety creeping in I would give myself Reiki. All my horrible memories would float away and any emotional attachment to them would dissipate. It was a wonderful time.

My life really stepped up a notch or two. I became a healer. The internet was just catching on and I would give distant healing and readings for people. I was good at linking into people distantly where the physical person was not in the way. I could remotely view people's rooms, what they looked like, and where their ailments lay. I was no doubt, the wounded healer. My self-healing continued, with Reiki, meditation and crystals, lots of crystals!

Sadly my second marriage didn't last very long. When I started a University degree to study Biology, my Husband grew distant and eventually stopped talking to me. He would leave early in the morning, come home for dinner, go back out to work and come home late. Things fell apart. Once I finished my degree I left, and moved to Wiltshire, in the countryside, where I was once again happy.

I redeveloped my connection with nature, my inner journeying, communication with guides and spirits, and I developed Shamanically. This was where my heart lay. When I was connected with spirit, or out in nature, I felt whole and in the present, yet that moment was timeless. All my past hurts no longer existed. It was a natural state to be in.

Only when I was around people did those past hurts resurface. People constantly walked over me - now whether I am a gentle soul or not, no one should feel they have the right to do that. But it was the narcissists that I attracted, and anyone who has had experience of narcissists, knows they are very self-centred and unfeeling of others' emotions. It actually took another fifteen years to discover what a narcissist was. I researched the subject and soon realised that so many people in my life had been narcissists, beginning with my own Mother and Sister. No wonder I fell into their traps so easily; no wonder I had relationships and marriages with the wrong people. Men who pretended to be so lovely and perfect, then later showed their true personalities. Once I understood why these people continued to appear in my life, I was able to stop it from happening. I can now spot a narcissist more easily, with the help of my intuition, although it's not an easy task when they are so good at faking their personality, at least until you're hooked into their lives. Then they turn.

Now I know the patterns, I no longer give second, third or fourth chances to people. I suppose you could say that at long last I've learnt to set boundaries. Narcissists don't teach you to have boundaries, they don't allow you to have boundaries. They take and take and when you draw the line and say no more, they make you feel guilty and convince you that there's something wrong with you, that you're the selfish, inconsiderate one. After a lifetime of being treated in this way it's very difficult to re-programme yourself, but it can be done. Once you realise that you aren't the one that's insane, selfish, wrong or bad, you can rebuild a new confident, resilient new you.

I suppose what I'm saying in all this is that whatever happens in your life, whether good, bad, happy or sad (I think those are song lyrics!) it's all part of your personal development, your spiritual development, and it will all help you to realise what you like or dislike about your life, both past and present, how you want to live now and what you want to change. It is all down to you in the end. Notice the repeating patterns in your life, what supports you and what drags you down. Change those patterns, it isn't your destiny to suffer them, but to grow from them.

I believe my upbringing and my relationships with people have had a detrimental effect on my life, and it took me far too many years to figure it all out, but as soon as you come to the point where you can ask yourself, "Why is this happening? What do I need to learn?", then the answers start to flow into your life and changes can be made.

I am now three quarters of the way through my life (hopefully I have a few years left) and I often feel that time has been wasted. But during that time I have learned so much. You can't cut corners with life! What have I learned? Well, simply that when I'm in towns and cities I feel disconnected and out of balance, I become depressed. I have learned that when I'm around too many people I feel drained and agitated. I realise that when I am out in nature, I meld with it, become part of it, and my stresses, aches and pains subside. So, in my last remaining years on Earth I would love to spend more time with animals and less with humans.

I have reached the point where I wish to retire deep into the countryside, and look after animals that have been abandoned, abused or injured. So, I am currently organising a charity to help animals and I hope to open an animal sanctuary alongside a retreat centre, so that not only can the animals benefit from human care, but humans can visit and interact with the animals, which I believe will help them to reconnect with nature, and the divine, and remember who they truly are. It would be a healing experience for them, as well as the animals.

Humans live in concrete and brick artificial environments, which damages the soul. Humans need to spend time in nature, for true healing, otherwise they become drained of energy and become ill. Being in nature is like recharging your batteries. Spending time by the sea, rivers, mountains or trees, has an ionising effect on the body, removing negative energy and revitalising our natural energy core. This is so important for one to be healthy, and happy in life.

I would like to bring you a simple channelled message from my guides:

"My dear ones, understanding the connection you have with nature is important for the soul. When you are with other humans in a busy area, where many people are in a close proximity, it is natural for your energy and your aura to contract. You pass so many strangers in the street, or deal with them at work, your aura shrinks. This is not a beneficial state to be in for long periods of time. You become disconnected and depressed. So, if you can go to places where there are fewer people, preferably out in nature, your aura and energy field will naturally expand.

Your aura can expand up to a great distance, which is why you will feel a part of the natural environment that you are in. You feel connected because you *are* connected. Your energy merges with the energies of the trees and the flowers, with the animals, the rocks and the plants, and you are truly connected as one. This is a natural state for you to be in and you need to experience this as much as possible.

Find a place nearby where you can do this, where you can sit quietly and peacefully and reconnect with nature. For some it is not always easy to get out into the countryside but there may be other places where you can sit. There might be a quiet corner of a park, you may find you have a favourite tree that you can sit by, or maybe a quiet place by a canal or river. You may be lucky enough to have a sheltered, peaceful garden.

Any time spent in nature is beneficial to you, and spending time alone, or with close friends or family when out in nature is very beneficial. Take your children to the woods, take your dogs to the river, step out of your everyday commitments, reconnect with nature and feel the healing that this will bring you. If you are unable to get out into nature, then close your eyes, imagine a beautiful place in your mind, with trees and flowers, a flowing river, a blue sky, and allow your energy to fill this image and this will bring you inner peace and healing.

Always take time to relax and recharge. People often push themselves and push themselves, with no rest, working hard or helping others, often putting others, their friends and family, before themselves. You need time to rest and recuperate, to recharge your batteries, recharge your energy, and you will find your life much easier. And you will find inner peace, you will find inner calm and clarity for your purpose, and when you find inner peace and clarity within, your outer world will reflect also that peace and clarity".

Humans reside on this planet as an interconnection between spirit and earth. It is what brings life to the planet. Many people have lost their connection with the Source, they have lost their purpose for being and with that comes anxiety and depression. Connect with nature as often as you can. Breathe in the fresh air, smell the flowers, the trees and the damp earth beneath your feet. Listen to the flowing rivers and the wind in the trees. Listen to the birds in conversation. See how content you will feel and make it a regular part of your routine. Breathe life back into your soul, and bring soul back into your life.

Love and blessings to you all.

-End-

GOING FORWARD NOT BACKWARD
By
Debs Tye-Duck

Being at Primary School back in the early 70's, my Parents had been asked by my teacher Miss Spackman to come in and see her. Apparently it transpired that I couldn't read and that Miss Spackman had delivered a verdict to my Mother that I was apparently 'backward'. Well I did love nibbling the dog biscuits that were supposed to be used for counting while I daydreamed looking out the window!

My heartbroken Mummy cried all the way home, never forgetting the words that Miss Spackman uttered that day, and being a very determined Mother had me reading my Janet and John books.

A memory that I never forgot as I grizzled and sobbed trying to read the stories and adventures of Janet and John. The words so hard to understand and my tears squirting outwards like a clown was rather amusing to my Mummy, but Mummy was determined I was not going to be 'backward'. Being extremely intuitive to find what I was good at, a big drawing pad made from computer paper was hand woven by Mummy and bright coloured pencils put into my hands. This was the beginning! I drew many weird and wonderful pictures of Easter eggs, pictures of witches on broomsticks and family portraits.

That was the beginning of my childhood which propelled me into lots more drawings from books of dinosaurs and pictures of Victorian ladies from my prose book. Sewing and knitting and being so happy in being creative that when I was at secondary school the big question on Mummy's lips was, "What are you going to do when you leave school?" After much thought and contemplation, I was going to join the army, be an architect and many other big ambitious professions.

Then one day Mummy said to me "Debs you are not academic why don't you become a Nurse or a Hairdresser?" Hmmmmm…

So I thought very hard, well I thought to myself I don't like blood so being a Nurse was not enticing to me, so I will become a Hairdresser! The first day I started at the hair salon was so surreal, because I had never been to one in my life!

Over the next two years of pursuing my ambition of being a hairdresser I cried an awful lot and felt that I would never be any good. However, I slowly kept going and I remember the day I 'got it', cutting hair at different angles, and understanding shapes and styles. Not being content with being average I excelled and started to really enjoy my career which took me far and wide working in the hair salon on cruise ships. Working at my craft after 22 years, I started to feel no sense of purpose in my life, and for several years mooched about dragging my feet.

My journey started to feel exciting again when I started my own business and I opened the doors to my very own hair salon! It was fantastic, I felt alive again and even on my first day of opening where my stomach was churning and I was terrified, I did what I normally do and just kept on going!

As I stated I am not at all academic and Maths and accounts were terrifying but with some help from kind people I did manage to do the sums. In fact, I was determined the salon was going to be built on success in all aspects of financial, creativity and customer service.

Six months after it opened, the salon won the town of Trowbridge's 'Service Excellence Award' and many people were happy for us and many thought we did not deserve it so early on.

If I was ever going to say something that would inspire a person, it is to 'keep on going'. Mistakes are made and I made quite a few, but I learned. Have faith in yourself and don't let anyone tell you that you are something that you are not. Lucky for me Mummy didn't believe Miss Spackman that I was 'backward'. Mummy had faith in me that I would do something with my life. Nothing can hold you back you know. Most important to this little story is the faith I had in myself.

-End-

QUOTES BY CATH B
By
Cath B Akesson

A woman once said, "When I'm feeling down I read a lot of your quotes and they help me to keep my head up, and keep me moving on in a positive light." I feel that is the reason why quotes and sayings can help you, and that is why I am so passionate about writing them.

I feel that the written word is so powerful, and a quote can inspire you, encourage you as well as give you strength and courage when you go through difficult times. Sometimes a quote can show you that you are not alone.

I hope that you have enjoyed my quotes throughout this book; here's another:

"As of today; do not look back nor feel any regrets. Because regardless of the obstacles, or the circumstances that you have faced; they have led you to this particular moment. They were necessary for your inner soul to grow, and for seeing things in a different perspective. Accept what has happened and embrace your new beginning. You now have a fantastic chance to start over."

*"Be patient and do not rush. Do not push.
You do not have to search for your
purpose in other people or locations. Your
purpose is you. It has always been you.
Close your eyes, be still and go within; ask
her
questions, listen to her; she is ready to
provide you with the answers that you
seek."*

Cath B

RESOURCES

The Authors who have brought you their stories in this Anthology have all found themselves in challenging places, just like you most likely. If you resonate and would like to connect with any of them, please feel free to use their contact details below, along with the resources they have provided.

1. YOU ARE A HEALER By Sam Lyndley
   http://www.samlyndley.com
   http://www.facebook.com/discoveryourpurpose

2. GRIEF, DEPRESSION & ANGER – HOW I WORKED THROUGH MY PAIN By Andrea Nicole
   http://www.andreanicole.co.uk
   http://www.compellingwriting.co.uk
   http://www.smartcopywriter.co.uk
   http://www.discoveryourpurposeanthology.co.uk
   Facebook: @EmotionalIntelligence999
                    @Compelling Writing Limited
                    @AndreaNicoleSmart

3. WALKING WITH THE SPIRIT WORLD... BE THE BEST VERSION OF YOU By Mitch Garlington
   http://www.mitch-garlington.co.uk
   Facebook: @MitchGarlingtonMediumTarot

4. A JOURNEY THROUGH DEPRESSION By Anne Dickson

5. BACK FOR GOOD By Donna B
   Personal Website: http://www.donnab.co.uk
   Facebook: @3DonnaB

   Business Website: http://wwwwomenofpurposefoundation.com
   Facebook: @4womenofpurpose

6. THE NAME OF THE ROSE By Wendy Salmon
   http://www.wendysalmon.com
   Book currently available on Amazon:
   On the Path to Love – A Book of the Heart
   Coming soon: A Book of the Soul

7. A JOURNEY OF COMPASSION By Linda Sands
   Facebook: @atbcoaching

8. THE REMEMBRANCE OF THE SOUL By Tamlyn Jayne Wolfenden
   Facebook: @soulalignedfitness
               @modernmysticgoddess

9. THE MISSING PIECE By Vicki Briant
   Join my closed infertility group offering support and a safe place
   to discuss your own journey at:
   https://m.facebook.com/groups/344056496044809
   Follow our travels around Europe at:
   https://m.facebook.com/ourmapofdreams/
   http://instagram.com/ourmapofdreams/
   Our travel blog:
   http://www.ourmapofdreams.com/

10. DISCOVERING MY PURPOSE By Jo Gomme
    http://www.jogomme.com
    Facebook: @jojosenergy

11. LOSS & ANXIETY LED ME TO MY PURPOSE
    By Rachel Pernak-Brennon
    http://www.eibotanicals.co.uk

12. HEALING THE PAST TO CONCEIVE A MIRACLE By Becky Jones

13. ADOPTION AND ABANDONMENT By Linda Chester
    linda.chester@icloud.com

14. CONVERSATION WITH MY GODDESS ENERGY (GE)
By Linda C.
http://www.facebook.com/linda.chester.581

15. NOBODY LISTENS TO ME By Linda Chester
http://www.springmoorsanctuary.co.uk

16. FOR MY DAUGHTER By Lynsey Doel

17. SACRED WOMEN By Lynsey Doel

18. REIKI AND ME & MEDITATION FOR LETTING GO By Jo Prince
Facebook Groups:
Reiki – Physical, Emotional, Mental and Spiritual Well-being
Jo's The Body Shop At Home

19. HOW TO SHIFT FORWARD INTO BEING YOUR TRUE SELF,
RELEASING OLD PATTERNS OF BEING - Taking Care of Yourself
from the Inside Out - A Beginning By Jayne Turner
http://www.holisticcounselling.org
Email: jtholisticcounselling@gmail.com
https://www.amazon.co.uk/Little-seed-Jayne-Catherine-Turner
'The Little Seed' is available to buy on Amazon.
The story is about recognising our need for connection with
ourselves and others. It's the journey of self-acceptance, love,
belief and value and totally fits with my ethos of holistic
counselling.

20. INNER CALM By Jacquelina Wood Haskuka
I am an English artist on a wellness journey, helping people to
find their own inner calm and happiness using art, writing,
crystals, organic aromatherapy and nature.
Email: Jacquelina_Wood@hotmail.com
Facebook: @JacquelinaArt
Instagram: @JacquelinaArt

21. THE LOVE CHILD By Lady Jasmine Moorhouse 'Spirit Worker'
    Facebook: @ladyjasminehealing

22. MY CHAKRA JOURNEY OF DEEP HEALING AND TRANSFORMATION
    By Carol Boyes

23. MY WOMB STORY by Carol Boyes
    For more information about Carol's Chakra Bootcamp
    Programmes or any of the services she offers.
    Email: Carolboyes@live.co.uk
    Mobile: 07821 046383
    Facebook: @DivineAngelicChakra

24. PICTURE YOURSELF IN A BOAT ON A RIVER By Edna Clark
    Facebook: @otherworldcreations

25. THE GIFT OF LIFE by Amanda Thomas
    The House of Harmony
    For further information, advice or support:
    Sexual Abuse – www.safeline.org.uk
    MRKH Syndrome - www.mrkh.org.uk
    Endometriosis - www.endometriosis-uk.org
    PCOS – www.verity-pcos.org.uk
    Pituitary Gland Tumour – www.pituitary.org.uk
    Surrogacy - www.surrogacyuk.org
    Coeliac Disease - www.coeliac.org.uk

26. THE GIRL IN THE DARK By Lex Envy
    http://www.lexenvy.com

27. THE NIGHT I FELT I LOST EVERYTHING! By Victoria Baker
    http://www.facebook.com/VictoriaAnnCrafts
    http://www.facebook.com/EnergySignaturewithVictoria

28. OH HOW IT FEELS By Andrew Rowles

29. LIGHTWORKERS UNITED By S.A.M.
    Facebook: @suemugford.healinghands (The Reiki Cabin)
    Coming soon: Heaven Holds Our Hand

30. WHAT I DID WHEN I WAS TOLD I WAS NOT GOOD ENOUGH
    By Carolyn Louise Pearse
    Facebook: @carolynlouisebranding

31. RETURNING TO ME By Lizi May Davis
    Facebook: @lizisfitplace

32. MY JOURNEY; PERFECTLY IMPERFECT By Donna-Michelle
    Facebook: @clevercatbeadhappy (Handmade Jewellery)

33. JOURNEY OF THE WHITEBEAR By Evelyn Whitebear
    www.facebook.com/beast.haven
    www.evelynmw.wixsite.com/beast
    Instagram: beast.heaven
    www.heartsong.space
    www.whitehorsetattoo.co.uk
    Instagram: evelyn.whitebear_tattoo.artist
    www.facebook.com/WhitebearMandalaArt
    Instagram: heart.song.art

34. GOING FORWARD NOT BACKWARD By Debs Dye-Tuck
    Facebook: @debsmedium

35. QUOTES By Cath Akesson
    http://www.cathb.co.uk

DISCOVER YOUR PURPOSE HEALING & HOLISTIC FAYRE

First the Book, Now the Event
Come and Meet the Authors

Raising Awareness for the Mental Health Foundation Charity

SUNDAY 29TH APRIL 2018
11am-5pm Free Entry

Leigh Park Community Centre
Leigh Park Way
Westbury, Wilshire
BA13 3FN

Hosted by Mitch Garlington - Spiritual Medium/ Psychic / Tarot Reader

Come along and soak up the Energy…Healers…Spiritual & Psychic Mediums…Tarot…Crystals…
plus so much more.

"A Place to Grow from Pain to Purpose"

https://www.facebook.com/events/911954642294397

ABOUT THE AUTHORS

Sam Lyndley is an Intuitive Mentor, Healer and Sensitive who's passionate about guiding and supporting her fellow women in reconnecting with their purpose in a bigger way!

She 'woke up' to her spiritual 'goodness' at the age of 18 but stayed pretty much in denial until her late twenties, at which point she started questioning literally everything in her life and quickly realised she was living a big fat juicy LIE.

She thought that being happy meant having a nice car, home or holiday, BUT deep down, the truth was that she was miserable, unfulfilled and living in total chaos.

Luckily, she was 'awakened' when she attended a demonstration of mediumship and the medium called her out and said, 'You're a healer' – three words that changed her life forever!

THIS WAS HER WAKE UP CALL! So she started undoing all of the fakery and began a journey of self-discovery, peeling back layer after layer of pain, guilt and shame. She realised this was all a story – a story she'd created at a very young age – the story of 'I'm not good enough.'

Like many of us who are drawn to heal our 'stories,' Sam was called to step into the shoes of a healer and at last, she felt like she had finally arrived home. There was no more trying to fit in – SHE WAS IN! This was her home and from this place of safety, she decided to call in her own tribe; other Healers, Sensitives and Intuitives who just like Sam, felt called.

So at this point on her journey, the parts of her that had been asleep for many years slowly AWAKENED, and she began to remember who she truly was and why she was here – the question all females have!

Her authentic self had been truly hidden and as she reconnected to her inner wisdom, her calling became clearer. She was here to awaken and heal others so they could indeed step into purpose!

Sam's intuitive, feminine energy led her back to her truth. From here, she unleashed her message, and it began to reach far and wide, touching her fellow sisters' wounds.

One by one, they were called in to heal their blocks, stories and patterns. Through their communicative energy, many of these beautiful souls adopted the 'feel the fear and do it anyway' approach and stepped up, shining their light out into the world and onto those in need.

These days her life is much more in flow – mainly as in she's not trying to be anyone else. "I'm just ME" she says, and being in this energy allows her to bring the gift of HER fully: with laser intuition and the ability to see others crystal clear.

≈

Andrea Nicole is a live-in Auntie to a teenager who lost his Mum to Cancer when he was just 10; the Nephew of Andrea's partner of just one year. Not able to have any children of her own, Andrea fervently wanted a child to love and after several miscarriages, a fertility consultant gave her the hard news that she would never bear a child. With hope in her heart for a full life in spite of her emptiness, she created a vision board upon which she placed children as a high priority. As a writer and storyteller, she couldn't have made this one up believably, but there it is. A child came into her life needing a Mother figure.

With a variety of commercial writing, marketing and business development roles under belt spanning 40 years, Andrea is finally branching out with a vision to help those with valuable life stories become published, so others can benefit from their experiences. And she credits a handful of people met over the past decade, for their nurturing support.

With a love for 'old-time' music, Andrea frequents dance halls where Rock'n'Roll, Rockabilly, Doo Wop, Blues, Cajun and Bluegrass fills the air. Being taught how to jive by her Mum when she was just 'a teenager in love', she loves to step out onto the dance floor for some energetic fun. With music dominating her heart and soul, she is also learning to play the fiddle.

Andrea's dream for the future is to live in the country on land where she can hold retreats for writers, whilst indulging in her love of cats. With another vision board in creation, that's sure to be on the cards. In the meantime, Andrea lives in leafy Surrey with her partner and his Nephew, pottering around in their well-tended garden, bird-watching and writing her stories, whilst teaching others to write theirs.

≈

Evelyn Whitebear is a spiritual artist, shamanic healer, sound therapist and empath. She creates energy paintings, angel and goddess paintings. Evelyn currently has a little centre in Hungerford where she holds groups and workshops in mediumship development, channeling, dotwork mandala painting, drum painting, psychic development and healing, among others. Evelyn also gives Sound baths with singing bowls and gong.

Evelyn has a tattoo studio and has been a tattoo artist for many years. Currently creating mandalas and other designs for a second adult colouring book, Evelyn is a true artist. (The first book is already available from Amazon).

Evelyn believes that her purpose in life is to help people connect with their own spirituality, their inner god or goddess, and she holds a sacred space for them to do this, through sound, meditation, channelling and art, and also through connecting with nature and animals.

Evelyn is currently in the process of creating an animal sanctuary, as working with animals is where her heart truly lies. She is currently looking for suitable premises and land where her animals can enjoy the care and protection Evelyn is committed to give. There will be a spiritual temple alongside the sanctuary, and there will also be shamanic retreats organised to help support the project. Evelyn is currently setting up a charity to help to create and run the sanctuary, and has supporters and donators already. There is a website and Facebook page dedicated to the sanctuary, BEAST haven; the Best Exotic Animal Sanctuary & Temple.

Her lifelong dream is to work with elephants, and is planning to visit an elephant sanctuary in Thailand, where she can work with, and study, Asian elephants. A small proportion of the donations for BEAST will be sent to the elephant sanctuary to help the wonderful work they do rescuing ill-treated elephants.

≈

NOW…

Please visit our website for events and newsletters:

http://www.discoveryourpurposeanthology.com

AND…

You may have purchased this book through Amazon, in which case, you will have completed a 'Verified Purchase'

A Verified Purchase will enable you to leave a review on Amazon, which will help 'window-shoppers' find our book, which we trust will help them deal with their own issues. You can help others just by reviewing this book, if you wouldn't mind please. 😊

"She decided to move on, because she would rather be alone, than in a relationship with no love, respect or communication."

Cath B

"She finally saw her worth;
she listened to her soul
and she moved on."

Cath B